Original Sin in the
Twenty-First Century

Original Sin in the Twenty-First Century

RICHARD J. COLEMAN

WIPF & STOCK · Eugene, Oregon

ORIGINAL SIN IN THE TWENTY-FIRST CENTURY

Wipf & Stock
An Imprint of Wipf and Stock Publishers
199 W. 8th Ave., Suite 3
Eugene, OR 97401

www.wipfandstock.com

PAPERBACK ISBN: 978-1-6667-0466-2
HARDCOVER ISBN: 978-1-6667-0467-9
EBOOK ISBN: 978-1-6667-0468-6

08/06/21

Scripture quotations are from the New Revised Standard Version (Oxford
University Press, 1989)

Contents

Acknowledgments

I REMEMBER SO WELL my first classroom discussion on the book of Romans with J. Christiaan Beker, professor of biblical theology at Princeton Theological Seminary. He began by reminding us that St. Paul was the first Christian theologian, and armed with that insight, a new door opened on how to interpret all of Scripture. Now many years later, I find myself writing a book about original sin by way of St. Paul and Professor Beker. I trust I have not failed them now.

I lead a bi-weekly Bible study using the lectionary as our texts. For a number of years, participants have heard me briefly discuss a contemporary book about original sin. I am pleased that they will now be able to read the fruit of *our* discussions. My special thanks to Paul Ackroyd and Elizabeth Elliot for reading an initial draft.

Preface

"HOUSTON, WE HAVE A problem" (from the movie *Apollo 13*). Christians, we have a problem. No one is listening to us when we talk about original sin. Since I am the one declaring there is a problem, then I bear the responsibility to define the problem and address it. So I begin by stating what this book is not and what it is.

What this book is not: it is not my intention to add yet another exposition of either the history of original sin or its biblical meaning. This has been accomplished more than adequately by Tatha Wiley, *Original Sin: Origins, Developments, Contemporary Meaning* (2002), and Mark S. Smith, *The Genesis of Good and Evil: The Fall(out) and Original Sin in the Bible* (2019). Alan Jacobs, professor of the humanities at Baylor University, wrote an intriguing book about the cultural history of original sin. As he understands the task of writing about original sin, one begins confessing it as a provocative idea—a provocation that is located in its combination of repulsiveness and explanatory power. While his observation that original sin is a puzzle that we cannot unravel and yet cannot kill is true enough, I shun the proposition that we are stuck with a paradox that can only vex us. To be fair to Jacobs, he does prefer the description of provocation and argues that "we have never had more need to explain ourselves to ourselves."[1] On the other hand, I have taken upon myself the obligation to use the explanatory power of theology to end this book with the admonition to be vigilant.

What this book is: broadly speaking, this book is intended to guide the reader in rethinking original sin in the twenty-first century. In particular, and to the extent that original sin tells us something important and necessary about human nature, my goal is to clarify what constitutes our essential self, a self that is so *fundamental* that it is universal, inexorable, and holistic. Universal refers to human characteristics that are found without exception for our species. Inexorable refers to something that is beyond our control, something less than instinctual but more than incidental. Holistic refers to an overall methodology that pays attention to all three integrated aspects of being human—body, mind, and spirit. This becomes the first step toward defending the argument that the word original can and should refer to something that is enduring. See chapter 1, "Truths that Endure—Reframing the Issue."

The language of original when associated with sin and stemming from a biblical context almost always refers to the Adam and Eve narrative. While the debate about how to interpret these first chapters in Genesis continues, my intention is to leapfrog over the commonplace questions about the author's intention—literal, historical, symbolic, mythical, legendary, typological, or analogical issues—and focus on the theological truth/s embodied in that narrative. In a previous book, *Eden's Garden: Rethinking Sin and Evil in an Era of Scientific Promise*, I directed our attention to the proposition that Adam and Ever were being tempted by a world of possibilities that comes with knowing all things (the tree of the knowledge of both good and evil) and thus becoming all-powerful, like God. Their primal sin may have been disobedience, but their enduring sin is wanting it all. In addition, for *original sin* to have legs in a world where truth itself has been thoroughly secularized, it must refer to something about human nature that is embodied; and if embodied, then it has an evolutionary history. Thus, I assume the obligation to explore the evolutionary roots of original sin utilizing a number of disciplines that are not theological. See chapter 2, "A Biblical [Revisionist] Understanding of the Adam and Eve Narrative."

In order to fully explicate our essential self, a second requirement seems necessary. For the most part, original sin describes the human condition within a theological context, and this is especially true when that atoning work of Christ is included in the discussion.

In other words, my intention is to ask whether original sin as a description of human nature still makes sense apart from its Christian framework of sin and redemption. See chapter 3, "The Doctrine of Original Sin—What It Really Means."

As one of the major religious traditions of the world, Christianity is known to have the darkest understanding of human nature. The question is not only if it is unwarrantedly dark but dark enough when we include evil. The traditional interpretation of the doctrine of original sin has a way of unduly restricting our vision to black and white *sins* that in turn allow us to neglect the kind of *sin* associated with systematic dehumanization and willful ignorance. When we confess sins of commission and omission, we are still likely to omit the kind of evil that thrives on apathy and complicity. See chapter 4, "How Dark is Dark Enough?," and chapter 7, "The Challenge of the Twenty-First Century," where the context requires us to reimagine what it means to love our neighbor and serve God in an age of techno optimism and climate change.

I discovered that as my thinking about original sin progressed, something important had been omitted. Original sin needed a counterweight. Otherwise, it becomes a teaching that is inclined to distort a holistic understanding of our essential self.

It was tempting to rely on the theology of "created in the image of God" (*imago Dei*), because the logic is compelling: if every human being is created to reflect the goodness and beauty of God, then a balance is established. But there is no narrative of how an original goodness was lost or how it was restored by the saving work of Jesus Christ. And depending on your interpretation, *imago Dei* is constricted by its focus on human beings. The upside of an enduring truth about original goodness is knowing there is a goodness that cannot be taken from us, that it endures no matter what humans do or do not do. It endures, in fact, whether human beings still inhabit this planet. See chapter 5, "Original Goodness."

Like no other theologian, Reinhold Niebuhr was a realist; he recognized that we are not as good as our ideals, especially so when you are among the power brokers. The theological foundation he laid down in *The Nature and Destiny of Man* anchored original sin in the nexus of freedom and finitude—freedom to be whatever we can imagine and finitude in the evil we do in spite of our best intentions. Consequently, Niebuhr's realism is proving to be more valuable in the twenty-first century than the twentieth. See chapter 6, "Reinhold Niebuhr—Then and Now."

If it hasn't already happened, we are close to a *fait accompli.* Original sin can now be found in the trash bin of irrelevant truths. In order to resurrect this enduring truth, the context must include three transformative revolutions that already engulf this century. The day is coming when all or most of us will be living with *modified genes,* modified by human intervention rather than random selection, and thus offering the opportunity to engineer our dreams and our desires. *Artificial intelligence* is already opening doors we never envisioned. It is already everywhere, becoming omnipotent and omnipresent. But along with each technological advance comes a host of unintended consequences (cyber warfare, a venue to spread lies, etc.). As the earth warms and *climate change* becomes a reality, we will find ourselves asking why didn't we do more, sooner. See chapter 7, "The Challenge of the Twenty-First Century."

There is another question you may be asking: why this book now? These harbingers of change refer to a century where the hand of man will be everywhere, otherwise known as the Anthropocene Era. What these transformative events have in common is the way they place human beings at the epicenter of how they will unfold. Spurning Mother Nature and beginning the process of evolving ourselves genetically means we become responsible for what we will become. To the degree that we write the code for artificial intelligence, we will be shaping AI in our own image. Global warming is nothing more and nothing less than what we have done and what we will do. Thus, the hand of human beings will be the deciding factor. Unless we be vigilant, we will learn once again that our ideals will not save us.

Lastly, a personal note. I accept the challenge to write about an *ancient* theological doctrine at a time when the world is convulsing during an insidious disregard for truth and the COVID pandemic. My effort would be amply rewarded if someone wrote book review that began: "I did not believe anyone could write something stimulating and relevant about original sin. I was wrong. The author quickly convinced me the twenty-first century is both an opportunity and an imperative to do just that."

FRONT MATTER ENDNOTES

1. Jacobs, *Original Sin*, xvii.

Chapter 1

Truths that Endure— Reframing the Issue

THE BLATANT PROPOSITION I proffer is to think of original sin as belonging in the pantheon of enduring truths. If enduring means hanging in there till the bitter end, then original sin qualifies. But that is a minimal qualification. One must also ask if original sin has explanatory power. And finally we must consider if it is knowledge that leads to wisdom, for wisdom endures in ways that knowledge does not.

Alongside these claims for original sin is the even more audacious proposition that theological truths endure because they reveal something about the meaning of life that cannot be captured by empirical knowledge. While both empirical truths and theological truths share the characteristic of enduring, they have endured for very different reasons, since they are very different kinds of truth. I trust this will become clear as we proceed.

The motivation that drives this book then is a rethinking of original sin in an era obsessed with knowledge that brings some economic benefit. This has happened at the expense of truth that invites us to ask questions that can be addressed only with language. Theological truths have suffered the consequence of becoming irrelevant, because the truth about our true nature as human beings can be painful. The telling consequence of having only one gold standard for what counts as rational knowledge is to presume that theological truths are not only irrelevant but specious. When theologians even begin to ask what enduring truth might be found in original sin, they are required to provide some kind of empirical evidence. Fortunately, original sin is about human behavior, which we witness on a daily basis. To the extent that there is a pattern of behavior that is universal and enduring, the conversation becomes of great import.[1]

The intent of Yuval Noah Harari's second blockbuster book, *Homo Deus,* was to describe in broad strokes the general direction of history in the twenty-first century, a century where we acquire for ourselves "divine powers of creation and destruction, and upgrade *Homo sapiens* into *Homo deus*."[2] (Harari's first hugely popular book was *Sapiens: A Brief History of Human Kind,* 2015). And how will we do this? With the ability to re-engineer our bodies and minds in order to escape old age, death, and misery; to make us better than what nature gives us; to transform data into knowledge where it can be used to develop technologies that will make a few of us a lot of money.[3] But Harrari also asks, "Can someone please hit the brakes?"[4]

And who is that someone? Harrari provides a helpful observation that it will probably not come from religion. Religions, he argues, will become simply irrelevant when they lose touch with the technological realities of the day and thereby "forfeit their ability even to understand the questions being asked."[5] What will be their answer, Harari asks, when artificial intelligence outperforms humans in most cognitive tasks? "Radical Islam," he observes, "may promise an anchor of certainty in a world of technological and economic storms—but in order to navigate a storm you need a map and a rudder rather than just an anchor."[6]

While it is certainly true that religion can be both a creative and a reactive force, there is an argument to be made that Christian theology is obligated to do exactly what science is neither prepared nor obligated to do, namely, to inquire after meaning. It can also be argued, and should be argued, that since the technologies of the twenty-first century will include the potential for great good and great harm, we will be confronted with an increasing number of life-and-death decisions. Thus, this runaway train not only needs an engineer it needs a engineer prepared to slow down when there is a yellow caution light flashing. This engineer could be theology armed with the enduring truth of original sin.

The picture of a runaway train without an engineer is a vivid image of how we feel about technology. And it is certainly true that beginning in the twentieth century and accelerating into the twenty-first century, this train knows only one speed, and because of that it lacks direction. But when the train has an engineer who knows where the train is going (its purpose), it is the engineer who should concern us. My argument throughout the book is focused on human nature; that would be the engineer who wants to take charge of everything. Give me information about the engineer, and I have a good idea whether brakes will be applied and whether anyone is taking seriously the direction and the values a particular technology embodies.

"So the Internet Didn't Turn Out the Way we Hoped" is the title of a *New York Times Magazine* from 2019. Mark Zuckerberg and his Facebook empire had a very bad year or two. Criticism had been relentless—too big, too powerful, too everywhere, too naïve, too focused on growth at any cost. One of several contributors to the *Times Magazine* issue, Bill Wasik, comments that "after decades of imagining Facebook as a utopia and then years of seeing it as a dystopia, we might begin to see it for what it is, which is a set of powerful technologies in the midst of serious flux."[7] But artificial intelligence will always have an engineer, and it will always be us, because humans will be the ones who write the programs that become the instructions for whatever AI executes.[8] Evolving ourselves by manipulating our DNA, boosting our mental capacities, and enhancing our bodies with implants is far more consequential than asking Alexa to order something from Amazon. Global warming leading to climate change is the consequence both of our doing and our not doing. Artificial intelligence, evolving ourselves genetically, and global warming are the determinate revolutions of this century, because they will challenge us to be our best selves in ways we are only beginning to understand.

Stepping back to gain a little historical perspective, we see that theology and science are in a very different juxtaposition than at any previous time. There was a time—oh so long ago that we have forgotten—when theology was regarded as the queen of all intellectual domains, including law, poetry, geometry, astronomy, philosophy, and mathematics. These lesser disciplines served as her handmaidens, for she was the great integrator that possessed the most important knowledge of all—your salvation. To be an educated person (at that time exclusively a man), you went to the university and studied theology. The Middle Ages came and went. The Renaissance came and went. The Reformation came and went. The Scientific Revolution came and stayed.

By the time of his death in 1882, Darwin, along with Sir Isaac Newton, had created a new coherent worldview. Newton had consolidated the physical world governed by universal laws of motion and his mathematical description of gravity. Darwin accomplished a parallel consolidation of the biological world with his understanding of evolution. While Newton thought of himself as a religious person who dedicated his nighttime endeavors to searching the Bible for a secret key to unlock its mysteries, Darwin slid from Anglican believer to embittered agnostic. That in itself reveals where history was headed.

Darwin, though, was confronted by a problem that is still with us. How does a process that is blind and uncaring produce a species that is purposeful and caring? (Hardly your lilies of the field picture.) In addition, Darwin had the task of interpreting to the public a process that takes place over millions of years, is incremental, meandering, and imperceptible. What both natural philosophers, as they were known then, had in common was their confidence in a new way of knowing by means of careful observations to gather data in order to test a hypothesis, the use of mathematics and equations to describe the world, and a style of thinking that begins from the bottom up (data) rather than from the top down (revealed truths).[9]

Theology's dethronement was a gradual process, but it became matter of fact when science became an autonomous discipline ruling over its own domain. It not only claimed the superior methodology, it fueled a new economy dependent on each new technological innovation. Having become the gold standard of what counts as the kind of knowledge that matters, science is that to which we look, not religion or theology, to give us a better life, to feed the world, to take us on a journey into outer space. Scientists are invited to the White House to advise the president (President Trump being the exception). It is the National Academy of Science that receives federal money to the tune of billions of dollars, year after year. And why is this important? It demonstrates that in the twenty-first century theologians will struggle to be heard, while scientists create their own headlines of the next best thing. Science represents the hope of the future, but at the same time it also represents the worst that can go wrong (I am thinking of biological warfare, cyber disruption, etc.).

This book does not strive to be an example of interdisciplinary dialogue between science and theology. If that is what you are looking for, I direct your attention to the interdisciplinary problem of understanding human distinctiveness. J. Wentzel van Huyssteen's *Alone in the World?: Human Uniqueness in Science and Theology* is an admirable example of how this works. Here we find a rethinking of the *imago Dei* (of being created in the image of God) as a root metaphor for understanding what it means to be human as "embodied uniqueness."[10] "The defining notion of the *imago Dei* in theology," he writes, "will turn out to be an interesting and even tempting link to various notions of human uniqueness in the sciences."[11] I would argue, nevertheless, that what we also learn from this kind of interdisciplinary dialogue is the insight that theology and science are self-limiting by the methodologies that define them—thus my interest in pursuing a holistic understanding of human nature by allowing both disciplines to speak for themselves. There are many other disciplines and voices that I also include.

The twenty-first century is a new day for a new kind of language. It seems to me that there are significant reasons why the traditional language of original sin is out of place, so much so that I have felt the need to adopt a methodology and language that is not blatantly religious or even theological: our sinful self becomes our worst self, and created in the image of God becomes our best self. The knowledge of good and evil becomes our insatiable drive to know all things. Eve's overreaching becomes symbolic of our endemic discontent with just about everything—the color of our hair, our body shape, the way our day is going, the way politicians hold onto power for as long as they can, the way everything seems to be about money, and of course the weather, which has a new significance as global warming becomes climate change, and climate change becomes warmer oceans, more hurricanes, sweeping forest fires, and rising levels of water. Finding a new language, however, does not mean abandoning the language of sin itself, for as Barbara Brown Taylor points out in *Speaking of Sin*, abandoning the language of sin/s "will simply leave us speechless before them, and increase our denial of their presence in our lives. Ironically, it will also weaken the language of grace, since the full impact of forgiveness cannot be felt apart from the full impact of what has been forgiven."[12]

Adopting a new language is meant to further the discussion of what endures, what is universal, and what is inexorable about human nature, so that we find ourselves saying, "Nothing changes, while everything is changing." The twenty-first century requires us to be more intentional when we use the word evil. Not only is the word used indiscriminately, but more important is the question of whether we are encountering a form of human sin unlike anything we have experienced before (e.g., allowing the air we breathe to become polluted). When Darwin was considering whether human beings constituted a unique species, he did not take into account our capacity for unthinkable crimes against humanity. If he had, he might also have reconsidered what he thought about original sin. (He did not believe in it.) Who knows what else he might have wanted to rethink, if he had been acquainted with a contemporary theology of a suffering God. Here I have in mind Jürgen Moltmann's groundbreaking *The Crucified God*, where he established the cross as the foundation for Christian hope by inspiring us to reimagine God's suffering as an act of ultimate solidarity between God and humanity. As it was, Darwin could not reconcile for himself an omnipotent God who allowed his beloved daughter to die at a tender age.

Insofar as theology is defined by the power of word truths to change lives and change the world, it bears the mandate to be a prophetic voice. Christians have no monopoly on being prophetic. To the extent that anyone hopes to be a prophetic voice in the twentieth-first century, he or she can learn from Greta Thunberg, the sixteen-year-old schoolgirl from Norway as she stood before the Climate Action Summit of the United Nations (September 23, 2019). Listen to her and feel her outrage, her courage, her conviction:[13]

> We'll be watching you.
>
> This is all wrong. I shouldn't be up here. I should be back in school on the other side of the ocean. Yet you come to us young people for hope. How dare you!
>
> You have stolen my dreams and my childhood. And I am one of the lucky ones. People are suffering. People are dying. Entire ecosystems are collapsing. We are in the beginning of a mass extinction, and all you talk about is the money and fairy tales of eternal economic growth. How dare you!
>
> For more than thirty years, the science has been crystal clear. How dare you continue to look away and come here saying that you're doing enough, when the politics and solutions needed are still nowhere in sight, but everything is changing about the world around us.

After listening to this you may be reminded of Mic 2:1–3:

> Woe to those who plot evil,
> who have nothing better to do than devise wickedness!
> No sooner is it dawn and they do it,
> since they have the power to do so.
> Seizing the fields that they covet,
> they take over houses as well,
> owner and house they seize alike,
> the man himself as well as his inheritance.
> (translation my own, alongside *The New Jerusalem Bible*)

Looking forward to chapter 2, I begin with a few introductory remarks. Throughout decades of parish ministry and even during my formative years at Princeton Theological Seminary, I have been drawn toward developing hermeneutical (interpretive) principles that help the reader understand the Bible, which is after all a bewildering mix of genres. So often we find ourselves asking: is it fiction or nonfiction? Is it history or fable? Is it biography or autobiography? Is it an eyewitness report or a later reflection?[14] It would be helpful, therefore, if we could focus on just one primary hermeneutical question: what is the theological intention of the author? This question not only helps us connect the past with the present as an interpretive principle, but it underscores that the theological was almost always the fundamental intention of the author. So, whatever the literary form, the overriding motive was to communicate an enduring theological truth.

A careful reading of Gen 1–3 reveals two distinct creation narratives (see below). There are a number of ways to account for this, including the documentary hypothesis, which was first proposed by the German scholar Julius Welhausen around 1883. Since then, it has been the subject of great scrutiny, but its central thrust remains intact. In the Old Testament, one finds four distinctive traditions or theological perspectives.

1. The Yahwistic tradtion (J), so-called because its writers used the tetragram YHWH for naming God. (The German transliteration is Jahwe, and its equivalent in English becomes Jehovah.)
2. P refers to the priestly material where laws and cultic matters are a major concern.
3. The E redactor is so named after the use of Elohim for naming God.
4. The Deuteronomist tradition (D) includes the books of Deuteronomy plus Joshua, Judges, First and Second Samuel, and First and Second Kings.

It is valuable to remember that what we are actually reading is a stitching together of earlier texts that in turn depended on even earlier oral traditions. The difficulty that scholars encounter is trying to reach consensus about those texts that stich together several traditions. For my purpose, this controversy is not important. What matters is that we have two parallel accounts of creation by way of two identifiable theological traditions, the Yahwistic and the priestly traditions.

Beginning with this premise of two theological traditions, we are then prompted to ask why the final redactor included two creation narratives as his prelude to God's covenant with Israel that begins in Gen 12. The same question applies to why there are four Gospels and many other parallel accounts in both the Hebrew and Christian testaments. The obvious answer is that two theological perspectives are better than one, just as four Gospels are better than one. Robert Alter, professor of Hebrew and comparative literature at the University of California, suggests that the ancient Hebrew writers "were motivated by a sense of high theological purpose."[15] In particular, and with Gen 1–3 in mind, the biblical writers of the creation narratives were confronted with a difficult task. How does one write about the beginning of all things and the human condition in such a way that it becomes memorable?

Alter is also convinced that the biblical authors were impelled to use fiction or narrative because of the kind of knowledge it could impart. They became pioneers of prose fiction in the Western tradition because they understood the power of imagination. One should not be surprised then that in these opening eleven chapters, the narrator is omniscient and knows quite literally what God said and what God knows. In his important but little known book, *The Humiliation of the Word*, Jacques Ellul, the French sociologist and Christian apologist, makes an important distinction between two kinds of truths: the use of language to address enduring truths (word truths) and the use of language to describe a verifiable universe (empirical truths). The unique power of language comes from not being bound to reality or the obligation to describe reality historically or literally. The universe of word truths—poetry, origin stories, myths, parables, narratives—permits one to address those kinds of questions that can only be answered by way of word truths. When Ellul writes "the ultimate destination of a human being belongs to the domain of Truth," he has caught the driving intention of those who fashioned the Adam and Eve account.[16]

RECOMMENDED READING

Alter, Robert. *The Art of Biblical Narrative*. New York: Basic, 2011.

Coleman, Richard J. *State of Affairs: The Science-Theology Controversy*. Eugene OR: Cascade, 2014.

Harari, Yuval Noah. *Homo Deus: A Brief History of Tomorrow*. New York: HarperCollins, 2017.

Smith, Mark S. *The Genesis of Good and Evil: The Fall(out) and Original Sin in the Bible*. Louisville, KY: Westminster John Knox, 2019.

Taylor, Barbara Brown. *Speaking of Sin: The Lost Language of Salvation*. Cambridge, MA: Cowley, 2000.

Chapter 2

A Biblical (Revisionist) Understanding of the Adam and Eve Narrative

How true it is: "Few stories in the history of the world have proved so durable, so widespread, and so insistently, hauntingly real." So writes Steven Greenblatt in his sweeping book, *The Rise and Fall of Adam and Eve.*[17]

In the first creation account (Gen 1:1–2:3), God is the all-powerful Creator who brings order out of chaos and creates everything to be good. According to Alter's description, everything is beautifully choreographed in an orderly fashion, day by day, through a series of balanced pairings: the primordial light (day) from the primordial darkness (night), the upper waters from the lower, the sun by day and the moon by night, male and female. For the first four days of creation and before the creation of the animal realm, the governing verb is *to divide*, suggesting the writer experienced a world that is carefully balanced by oppositions.[18] While there is no specific mention of sin or evil, there is the ever-present threat of chaos overwhelming order. Evil, we could say, is not defeated but contained.

In this priestly account, the inherent goodness of creation spills over into the creation of humans, male and female. This narrator tells us next to nothing about what it means to be made in the image of God, for that is left to the second narration, where being alone is not a good thing, and being in relationship is a good thing. Here the humans are blessed and told to "be fruitful and multiply, and fill the earth and subdue it; and have dominion over the fish of the sea and over the birds of the air and over every living thing that moves upon the earth" (Gen 1:28). The use of words such as *dominion* and *subdue* have become troublesome for those sensitive to male domination and the integrity of all living things. But taken in context, the language is appropriate as long as we maintain a connection between humans being created in the image of God and the mandate given them. That mandate is to understand the land as a gift along with instructions for its good care. Ellen Davis, a theologian at Duke Divinity School, provides an even broader reading of the Bible. In her *Scripture, Culture, and Agriculture*, she reminds us that the covenant between God and Israel includes an ecological responsibility to honor the land (dirt) from which they came.[19] We might prefer a translation of the Hebrew words in Gen 1:26 and 28 to be something like "be responsible stewards" or "exercise loving care." But living in a world where food does not come pre-packaged, and life is ever so tenuous, subduing the world around us is what we have always done—until now, as we begin to understand the full consequences of an economy based on raping the Earth without any regard for God's living creatures. In addition, surprisingly so, the context is that while everything that lives needs to eat, there is no blood-letting. Everything and everyone is vegetarian ("and to everything that has the breath of life I have given every green plant for food"—Gen 1.29–30). So, dominion and subdue take on a more benign and realistic connotation than we usually presume.

Keeping in mind that this first account is a priestly narrative, we might be less surprised to read how it concludes. Framed by "in the beginning" and "thus the heavens and the earth were finished," the narration ends with "God blessed the seventh day and hallowed it" (Gen 2:3). We can poke fun at the thought of God resting, but it's a poetic way to emphasize the importance of the fourth commandment: "Keep the Sabbath as a holy day." The purpose of this first account then is to provide the ultimate basis for observing the Sabbath: six days you will labor, but on the seventh day, you will rest and remember your Creator. Furthermore, this world is a good creation, because it is God's creation, rather than something humans have fashioned with their own hands. So note that the fourth commandment is not license simply to rest but to end your day's work in order to be content with what is given, where you pause to give thanks for what you have and where all God's creatures have a foretaste of a peaceable kingdom.

In the priestly tradition, the answer to chaos is order, the answer to lawlessness is law, and the answer to being a faithful covenant partner with God is the commandments. When comparing this narrative to the next one (Gen 2:4–3:24), the ethos is static, reminiscent of the Great Chain of Being and reflective of a universe governed by immutable laws, where everything is perfect just as it is. There is nothing messy about this portrait, whereas the second narration is more anthropomorphic, psychologically dynamic, and descriptive of why this is not the best of all worlds.

The second narrative begins with a transitional statement, "when the Lord God made the earth and the heavens," but then steadily moves toward a more dire picture even before introducing Adam and Eve. Earth itself is barren and dry, anticipating a land filled with thorns and thistles. Poor Adam has no fit companion and is fated to return to dust. Rather than emphasizing the goodness of creation, the narrator refers to the possibility of temptation, for in this garden there is the tree of the knowledge of good and evil. While Gen 1 informs us how it all started, the Yahwistic writer provides an etiological explanation with respect to childbirth, marriage, and work and does so within a theological framework. Yahweh is mindful of murder (ch. 4) and a great evil that will require a flood to restart the human experiment (ch. 9). There is no hint of murdering another person in the first creation account, for everything is created good. Turn the page, and one finds the first episode of jealousy and anger leading to ending your brother's life. But there is also tenderness and love: "And they become one flesh" (Gen 2:24); "Adam knew his wife again" (Gen 4:25). Above all else, the Yahwistic story is about real life, real experiences, what it means to be morally responsible for one's actions, the reality of evil, and how to live faithfully when God seems all too absent (Yahweh speaking to Cain: "and I shall be hidden from your face" [Gen 4:14]).

In the garden of Eden—The Garden of Eden is a mythical place that invites more than just a little rumination. The Hebrew translation is "the garden of delights" and thus a place where temptation is nonexistent, because everything ever needed or wanted is there. There are no needful things, as Steven King depicts in his novel by that name where Satan, posing as a shopkeeper, makes bargains too good to pass up (and with deadly consequences down the road). So picture yourself in such a place, and ask yourself what life would be like without any challenges, without any goals for which to strive, without any disappointments, without even the dignity that comes from work and the miracle of birthing a child. Everything you ever wanted is within reach. Without even an inkling of discontent, Adam and Eve would know nothing of the joy of victory or the agony of defeat. What a life! The best of all worlds?

Surrounded by perfect love, perfect pleasure, and one perfect delight after another, what could they find disquieting? Well, there is that one injunction. Do not under any circumstances eat of the tree of the knowledge of good and evil and of the tree of immortality. Your horizon has just been limited. So, let's file that away as a limitation on what you might desire.

How fortuitous that the tree of knowledge in the garden of Eden was the object of their desire. That wily serpent spins a few lies and invites them to break bad, because they just might want a little more excitement in their lives. Boredom is no trifling condition for sin to germinate, for this is how we severely punish prisoners, by putting them in isolation cells. But breaking bad and being disobedient is only part of what happened in the garden of delights.

Picture yourself as the serpent—not just any serpent, but a talking one, bearing symbolic connotations of both good and evil from mythic stories and civilizations, primarily from Israel's neighbors of Egypt and Babylonia. This clever serpent knows how temptation works:

> The serpent begins by eliciting doubt about what God said: "Did God actually say eat of this fruit and you shall

die?" Sow a little doubt, then ask more questions. "How is it going, Eve? What a life. Everything you could want, everything within reach. One would think that you have it all. But do you? Yes, I have seen you and Adam pause to look at that tree, yes, the one in the middle of the garden. I have heard that it will give you knowledge of every kind, both good and evil, even wisdom, the crown of knowing. Could it be that you are just a tiny bit bored? You know, 'dear,' your horizon has been limited. Your idea of beauty has been cramped. There's an infinite cosmos out there you haven't even considered. Your mind—yes, your mind—is capable of so much creativity you can't even imagine. Perhaps, just perhaps, God has sold you short and cramped your style. You know, don't you, that you are capable of so much more? You think you have seen everything. Well, just wait until your eyes are open, really open. And I'll let you in on a little secret: you will not die if you reach out and partake."

Knowledge of good and evil—Why is knowing good and evil a forbidden fruit? The venerable Old Testament scholar Gerhard von Rad considered this is be a Hebraic expression for the totality of knowledge, for this is what makes mere mortals godlike.[20] Gen 3:22 makes that clear: "Then the Lord God said, 'See, the man has become like one of us, knowing good and evil.'" The narrator also makes a distinction between knowledge per se and knowledge that leads to wisdom, which is what true knowledge can become when we have not fallen from God's favor (Gen 3:6). It's an interpretation that is reinforced by the association with opening their eyes to a world of possibilities. And its associated with desire; the fruit is so intoxicating that it should not even be touched. In other words, it is the kind of knowing that is dangerous, more than humans can safely handle, and coupled with the tree of life, it is everything one needs to become godlike. This, Yahweh will not allow.

In the image of God—These two words, *imago Dei*, have provoked a rich and diverse outpouring of theological discourse. Van Huyssteen, retired professor of theology and science at Princeton Theological Seminary, provides the following broad categories to explain what it means to be created in the image of God: *unique qualities* such as rational discernment, intellect, memory, language, and spirituality (Western theologians); *functionality* in the sense that God calls us to be caretakers and stewards of creation and to be deputized to speak for God as the prophets did (von Rad); *relational*, such as to be in relationship with God and with others (Robert Jenson, Karl Barth); *exocentricity or self-transcendence*, such as a disposition to be open to a world and a future that is always unfolding (Wolfhart Pannenberg); and *ethical awareness*, in the sense that we have awakened to our moral responsibility for all of creation (Van Huyssteen).[21] Nothing is said about a greater intellect or even a different kind of intellect. But in place of a discourse on the emergence of language or symbolic thinking, the biblical writers (J in particular) include a conversation between Yahweh and Adam. What this means theologically is that one of God's creatures and only one is distinguished by knowing the difference between existing and being created, that is, we are creatures who pray (and argue with God, as Judaism reminds us).

Each one of these approaches has something important to add to our understanding of *imago Dei,* but staying close to the first four chapters of Genesis, these salient features stand out.

- We are created male and female without distinction of value.

- We are not created to be alone but to be part of a community of living things.

- We are created with the freedom and the will to reach and to overreach, along with the ability to suffer the consequences for our actions.

- By knowing both good and evil, we find ourselves in a predicament: while we are not all-knowing, we are sufficiently self-aware to believe we are destined to be all-knowing and thus to begin to act as if we were all-powerful.

- Eve's overreaching symbolizes our innate propensity to desire all things but to be left feeling unfulfilled.

Overreaching—The wily serpent did not have to work very hard to persuade Eve to reach out her hand and take what was forbidden. Could it be that Eve had already been considering what it would feel like to have free reign to reach for what one desires? Desire is presupposed. Humans are made with a capacity for desire. "So when the woman saw that the tree was good for food, and that it was a delight to the eyes, and that the tree was to be desired to make one wise, she took of its fruit." (Gen 3:6). In Gen 2:9, God made the tree of life attractive and desirable. We are told the fruit is a delight to the eye; it must have had an allure like no other fruit. For good reason, then, the narrator couples both overreaching and desire. What prompts overreaching is the desire for something, and not just the desire for this or that but specifically the desire for something one does not have. What ultimately springs to life is an infinity of desires.

The pictorial image of Eve reaching is both graphic and compelling. So for centuries, how did we miss the implied meaning—not just reaching but overreaching?

Even though it is as old as Adam and Eve, in the twenty-first century, overreaching has a new meaning and a new context: overprescribing, overdosing, overfishing, overconsuming, over-fertilizing, overpromising, etc. In an age of unfettered capitalism and overconsumption, there is never enough. In *Homo Deus,* the acclaimed master of big history Yuval Harari writes: "Humans are always on the lookout for something better, bigger, tastier," and let's add for something faster and, of course, more data.[22]

Disobedience—What is disobedience if not the assertion of one's will? Your child's first emphatic *no* comes as a shock to most parents because it is a demonstration of "here I am, and I am asserting my will." As parents, we can respond either by thinking "this is my house and my rules," or "I understand how one develops from a dependent child to an independent adult." Likewise, we can read the Adam and Eve story in two ways. It would seem that in the garden of Eden (God's house), Adam and Eve are expected to listen and obey. They are just two immature human beings. Or Gen 3 can be read as a coming-of-age story. In one hesitant no (or was it an emphatic no?), Eve and Adam decide to enter the world where limits are not what life is for. Rather, a life fully lived begins with the freedom to decide and to live with the consequences. But in her innocence, Eve did not comprehend the consequences. Life outside of Eden will not only be burdensome, because life itself is difficult; it will also be a battle of wills between what we know we should do and wanting what we want now.

Well into the twenty-first century, we are no longer immature adolescents, for we have learned to direct our own evolution in order to seize the day and make ourselves better than what nature gives us. This is our moment, for our time has come. We are the adult now and no longer content with reminders about destiny, fate, or providence. Armed with an arsenal of technologies, we now have the tools for shaping the world in our own image and according to our own desires. When scientists and technocrats (not all but many) chafe at the idea of limits about what they should be allowed to know or do—because, after all, knowledge is considered to be at least neutral if not inherently good—they are forgetting that knowledge and wisdom are not the same.

Naked, ashamed, vulnerable—Whether a moment in history or a continuum of our evolutionary history, the symbolism is exquisite: the two of them standing there looking at each other and thinking, "What have we done!" Innocence is gone, and self-awareness has arrived. Artists have never yet failed to explore another emotion to depict. Was it shame or guilt that overwhelmed them? What was it like to be Adam and Eve before they became fully self-aware? Well, they had nothing about which to be ashamed, including their nakedness (Gen 2:25). But that changes after they succumb to the serpent's temptation. Adam says, "I heard the sound of you in the garden, and I was *afraid*, because I was naked; and I *hid* myself" (Gen 3:10; italics added). So what had changed? Was it as simple as finding ourselves with something to hide? See chapter 7.

The association of nakedness with shame and vulnerability is fairly obvious. We are the only creature that clothes itself and spends way too much money on being fashionable. Why do we act this way? Why do we regard our sexuality as sufficiently immoral that it needs to be covered up? We know why. The knowledge of good and evil, which has become an integral part of being fully human, spills over into everything, and most noticeably and troublingly because our sexual urges are so powerful that they threaten to undo our willpower to do what we know is right. The biblical writers are not reticent to remind us that the sordid account of David and Bathsheba was not an anomaly. Three chapters later, when the Genesis telling expands to include the world, we read: "When people began to multiply on the face of the ground, and daughters were born to them, the sons of God saw that they were fair; and they *took* wives for themselves of all that they chose" (Gen 6:1–2; italics added). Our nakedness symbolizes the end of innocence and the beginning of guilt betraying our no-good intentions. Shame and guilt, then, are the price humans pay for becoming so self-conscious that it leads to depression, suicide, paralysis, anxiety attacks, and a host of other self-inflicted disorders.

Being naked symbolizes real-life experiences of the vulnerabilities of being a body. Author of *The Roots of Morality* Maxine Sheets-Johnstone reminds us that rough-and-tumble play among humans and animals is a way of coming to grips with our vulnerability. It is a self-teaching exercise whereby we begin to learn limits and unintended consequences. But even after a lesson learned, one also learns to watch one's back and never be caught off guard, that is, to be found naked. And why is judgment day sometimes pictured as standing naked before God? Because we all have something to hide.

In *The Rise and Fall of Adam and Eve,* Stephen Greenblatt includes a chapter of theological questions that emerged when explorers from the Western world began to encounter naked natives, who were comfortable with their nakedness.[23] Sailing under the flags of Western civilization, one admiral recorded in his diary, "As naked as their mothers bore them; and the women also." Theological questions began to surface that did not have a satisfactory answer when we read the Genesis story absent a theory of evolution. How could an entire population, a population scattered across the unknown world, be exempt from the first consequence of the fall, namely, shame. "Shame," Greenblatt writes, "was not supposed to be a cultural acquisition; it was the inescapable, defining condition in the wake of sin."[24] Could it be that these natives in their bestial state represented a degeneration from the original goodness and perfection of Adam and Eve? Could they be inferior human beings living outside the garden of Eden?

While quite reticent to enter into this kind of theological nitpicking, Darwin, who had experienced for himself the shock of naked aborigines, had a very different response. Intent in defending his theory of evolution, Darwin confronted his own deep-rooted Victorian beliefs in a form of white supremacy by writing that he would rather "be descended from that heroic little monkey, who braved his dreaded enemy in order to save the life of his keeper . . . than from a savage who delights to torture his enemies . . . treats his wives like slaves . . . and is haunted by the grossest superstitions."[25]

Self-transcendence—The Adam and Eve story, and their temptation in particular, signals a capacity for self-transcendence. Self-transcendence is not only a capacity for self-reflection, but it also implies a predisposition to transcend our creaturely finitude. The divine image then implies a unique capacity to reach beyond the present moment, to sense there is something greater than oneself. The fact that we have a capacity for self-transcendence means we are not tethered to the here and now. This very capacity to transcend the present moment in turn incites a gnawing restlessness with being mere creatures. "For religious believers," Van Huyssteen writes, "it will be natural to interpret the emergence of consciousness and self-consciousness as revelatory of something deep in the universe, something inexplicable by physics, something behind the material face of the world."[26] This religious predisposition then is both a blessing and a burden: the blessing of our transcending the present moment and the burden of an unresolvable tension between our finite existence and our neverending-horizon existence. The Hebrew writers, however, show little interest in philosophical ruminations and are content to describe the holy Other as appearing "like a devouring fire on the top of the mountain" and bearing no name except "I am who I am" (Exod 24 and 3:14; cf. Isa 6).

The venerable and prolific Protestant theologian Karl Barth excelled in using language to remind us what constitutes being human when measured against the Creator.

> On the very brink of human possibility there has, moreover, appeared a final human capacity—the capacity of knowing God to be unknowable and wholly Other; of knowing man to be a creature contrasted with the

Creator, and, above all, of offering to the unknown God gestures of adoration. This possibility of religion sets every other human capacity also under the bright and fatal light of impossibility.[27]

Life and death—Saturating the first ten chapters of Genesis is the struggle of life and death, and when paired with the conflict between good and evil, they just about define what it means to be human. The denial of death predates the prehistoric cave drawings of Lascaux by thousands of years, and while those drawings mark a spectacular revolution in the human psyche, the denial of death and the hope for something better is far earlier if we consider intentional burials of an individual person.[28] While we do not know what motivated these early hominids, whether an act of remembrance or honoring the deceased, there came a time when preparing a tomb filled with items useful for an afterlife indicates the emergence of *Homo sapiens*. So, regardless of when it happened, it did happen, the emergence of a deep-seated hope for something beyond death.

There is nothing fuzzy about this aspect of the Adam and Eve narrative: death is our destiny, because it captures in no uncertain terms the tragic outcome of desiring to become godlike. Reinhold Niebuhr is especially insightful when he highlights the anxiety we experience when we believe we can transcend our human condition of finitude. In his reinterpretation of Gen 3, Adam and Eve become fully human when confronted with the final terror of self-consciousness, the knowledge of their mortality. Furthermore, Niebuhr's understanding of *Homo spiritus* explains why our will to be more than creature ignites a life of anxiety born of something that cannot be.[29]

Life in the twenty-first century does not require us to be fruitful and multiply—just the opposite. Our hope for an afterlife where we bury our loved ones with valuable treasures has been transformed by a growing practice of cremation, now approved by the Roman Catholic Church as long as it is not understood as a denial of our bodily resurrection. If we have arrived at a place where our heretofore denial of death has become the confidence that we can at least extend the span of our life, that may be enough to satisfy some of us but not all of us.

Original goodness—Contemporary biblical scholarship is quick to remind us that in the Adam and Eve story there is no language of original sin, for that is a later development dependent on integrating original sin into a doctrine of atonement.[30] But there are good reasons to find the seeds of a theology of original goodness in this prologue. For instance, Gen 1 explicitly emphasizes the goodness of creation prior to everything else. Thus one can conclude that sin and evil are unoriginal in that they disrupt a preexisting goodness. The Yahwistic storytelling also includes some good guys. Abel is a counterbalance to Cain, and after Cain comes Seth and Enoch, born "at a time when people began to invoke the name of the Lord" (Gen 4:26). Then when "the earth was corrupt in God's sight," God chooses Noah to build a salvation ark. After the flood recedes, God establishes a new covenant, which includes not only Noah and his descendants but "every living creature . . . as many as came out of the ark" (Gen 9:10). This covenant includes two conditions: you shall not shed flesh with its life, that is its blood and be "fruitful and multiply" (Gen 9:6–7).

The Genesis prologue of eleven chapters serves as a foundation for the epic story of a chosen people about to unfold. The prologue is prehistory or before time. Then in chapter twelve, Yahweh speaks to Abraham, and so begins the covenantal history of Israel. The injunction to be fruitful and multiply is itself a prelude to the covenant God makes with Abram: "I will make of you a great nation, and I will bless you, and make your name great, so that you will become a blessing" (Gen 12:2). In the Hebrew Scriptures, the universality of sin is not disputed, but the focus is not on original sin but the unresolvable struggle between two impulses, the inclination to do good, *yetser ha-tov*, and the inclination to do evil, *yetser ha-ra*. What endures for the Hebrew writers is not a fall from God's grace but the struggle to be a partner with God and to be a holy people, a light unto the nations.

If the cornerstone of original sin is the Adam and Eve story coupled with Paul's reference to Adam in Rom 5:12—"Therefore, just as sin came into the world through one man, and death came through sin, and so death spread to all because all have sinned"—then the cornerstone of original goodness is Gen 1, where God's creation—all of it—is not only good but very good. As emphasized by contemporary biblical scholars and theologians, Adam and Eve are not cursed by God. Their punishment is to be exiled and barred from the garden of Eden where the tree of knowledge stands along side the tree of life. Their exile is nothing less than a reminder that humans cannot be trusted when the temptation is to believe there are no consequences to overreaching.

"What is man that thou art mindful of him, and the son of man that thou dost care for him?" Marilynne Robinson remarks that a question "is more spacious than a statement, far better at expressing wonder."[31] Ps 8 answers its own question this way: "Man is crowned with honor and glory." The Hebrew Scriptures everywhere concede: yes, a people who worship idols; yes, a stubborn and rebellious generation; yes, those who hate the good and love the evil; yes, guilty but still bestowed with glory and honor.[32] Still more: Human beings are worthy of being given dominion over the works of thy hands.

Conclusion—The working thesis I have put forward is simply this: the biblical writers were motivated by a high theological purpose, and we should not be surprised that they begin this grand narrative with an enduring truth about human nature at its best and worst. Alter also calls our attention to why these ancient Hebrew stories seem so intensely alive both then and today, for "they make sense of human reality in the radically new light of the monotheistic revolution," and they ask what it means "to live with an a divided consciousness—intermittently loving your brother but hating him even more . . . stumbling between disastrous ignorance and imperfect knowledge . . . outwardly a definite character and inwardly an unstable vortex of greed, ambition, jealousy, lust, piety, courage, compassion, and much more."[33]

The knowledge or wisdom the biblical writers intended to impart is what we know as enduring truths, not just any kind of enduring truths such as scientific facts, but enduring in the sense that they have the quality of being revelatory. One sense of what the word revelatory means is from God, but this is just a generalization. To be specific, an enduring theological truth is one that carries the potential of asking the kind of question we cannot ask ourselves.

If one tries to tell oneself a joke in order to make oneself laugh, it doesn't work. The first and primary example from the Scriptures is God's question to Adam and Eve, "Where are you?" Not where are you hiding but from what are you hiding, what are you not telling yourself; not only what have you done but what are you going to do now. Then in the very next chapter, God's question to Cain, "Where is your brother?" God already knows the answer, as does Cain, but added to Cain's interior voice (conscience) is the voice of the Almighty, for that is always an inquiring voice not of our own making and not of our own volition.

RECOMMENDED READING

Alter, Robert. *The Art of Biblical Narrative*. New York: Basic, 2011.

Coleman, Richard J. *Eden's Garden: Rethinking Sin and Evil in an Era of Scientific Promise*. Eugene, OR: Cascade, 2014.

Greenblatt, Stephen. *The Rise and Fall of Adam and Eve: The Story that Created Us*. New York: Norton, 2017.

Jacobs, Alan. *Original Sin: A Cultural History*. New York: HarperOne, 2008.

Smith, Mark S. *The Genesis of Good and Evil: The Fall(out) and Original Sin in the Bible*. Louisville, KY: Westminster John Knox, 2019.

Van Huyssteen, Wentzel J. *Alone in the World?: Human Uniqueness in Science and Theology*. Gifford Lectures. Grand Rapids: Eerdmans, 2006.

Chapter 3

The Doctrine of Original Sin— What It Really Means

As noted above, the *doctrine* of original sin is not the subject of this book. Nevertheless, I believe the doctrine speaks to the human condition in ways that are both critical and relevant for the twenty-first century. With this in mind, along with a need to clarify what is the essential teaching of the doctrine, the argument here and throughout the book is the naked truth that human nature is now as it has always been. This is an argument aimed at the Enlightenment notion that human beings can change when they are enlightened. (Even though education can be transformative in many ways, it is arguable whether it changes human nature in a fundamental way. It's a question that is by no means settled.) For all of us living in the twenty-first century, the reigning presumption is that everything we need to know about what is true goes no further than knowing how to change the world to meet our needs and desires. Thus, the question here is what enduring truths can be found in the doctrine of original sin that reveal something we are likely to misinterpret and ignore as the century unfolds.

Christians do not have a definitive doctrine of original sin. What we do have are ecclesiastical pronouncements both in their original form and then in their revised form. They differ for a number of reasons: what was at stake at a particular historical moment, the continual need to be contemporary, and the thinking and rethinking by Christian theologians. In Tatha Wiley's book *Original Sin,* two motivations are discussed to explain why the Christian doctrine seemed necessary. The first was the need for "a compelling explanation of why humans beings are as they are and what they need," and the second was the necessity for a "unified framework that includes the atoning or redemptive work of Jesus Christ."[34]

One finds a number of questions and themes that continually surfaced as theologians developed a doctrine of original sin, and always in their purview was the meaning of original and the meaning of sin. Original implies something universal and inexorable. Before there was a possible explanation by way of evolution, the most direct path was a literal reading of Gen 3; that is, Adam and Eve were the original humans, and their transgression or sin was transmitted to all subsequent generations. Before our modern understanding of biology, theologians were necessarily left to speculate. Paul's declaration that "all have sinned and fall short of the glory of God" (Rom 3:23) was a direct reference to the Adam and Eve account. His interpretation of Gen 3 in Rom 5:12 was typological—"Therefore, just as sin came into the world through one man, and death came through sin, so death spread to all because all have sinned"—and became the standard explanation for the universality of sin. Given his historical moment, it is most likely that Paul was reading Gen 3 literally, with Adam and Eve as historical individuals. But making this supposition does not preclude the possibility that the original writer/editor of Gen 3 was motivated to write a symbolic narrative in order to transcend any given historical moment. In other words, what was necessary for Paul, the first Christian theologian, to draw a typological analogy—"Therefore just as one's man's trespass led to condemnation for all, so one man's act of righteousness leads to justification and life for all" (Rom 5:18)—was not necessary for the Hebrew theologian to write, "See the human has become like one of us, knowing good and evil; and now, he might reach out his hand and take from the tree of life" (Gen 3:22).

With our focus still on the meaning of original, there are many places to find a pronouncement or an argument by the Protestant Reformers. One place is the international Synod of Dort held in Dordrecht from 1618 to 1619 by the Dutch Reformed Church to settle a divisive controversy initiated by the rise of Arminianism. Voting representatives from eight foreign Reformed Churches attended, and together they agreed on a number of articles intended to clarify any lingering doubts about original sin, among other theological questions. Below is an article under the heading "The Third and Fourth Main Point: Human Corruption, Conversion to God and the Way it Occurs":[35]

> Article 2: The Spread of Corruption
> Human beings brought forth children of the same nature as themselves after the fall. That is to say, being corrupt they brought forth corrupt children. The corruption spread, by God's just judgment, from Adam and Eve to all their descendants—except for Christ alone—not by way of imitation (as in former times the Pelagians would have it) but by way of the propagation of their perverted nature.

Reinhold Niebuhr offers what seems to me to be a contemporary and existential understanding of original sin. When he set out to mount a new defense of original sin, he understood the necessity of anchoring sin in the human condition itself. Niebuhr chose not to read the relevant biblical accounts literally or as historical facts, but he does offer another interpretation. Niebuhr argues that sin is not inevitable because of a biological (genetic) defect but rather because each and every one of us is caught in the web of breaking bad. to state it differently, we sin, because we are born into a world where sin is our history. By redirecting the discussion away from individualistic sins and a literal reading of the fall, Niebuhr argues that history repeats itself, because human nature repeats itself. Niebuhr also cautions that "when the Fall is made an event in history rather than a symbol of an aspect of every historical moment in the life of humans, the relation of evil to goodness in that moment is obscured."[36]

In an equally innovative move, Niebuhr defines the human condition as our desire to transcend the creature we are. Self-transcendence, the most evolved form of self-awareness, gives us the ability to step outside the world of self. Armed with this understanding, Niebuhr asks an even deeper question: Can we transcend our finitude? That is, can we ever cease being humans who desire to transcend the very finitude that is the essence of being creature? The same drive or capacity that causes us to be incurably creative and discontent—always desiring to know more, be more, want more, have more—is the crux of who we are. In his own words: "The human spirit cannot be held within the bounds of either natural necessity or rational prudence. In its yearning toward the infinite lies the source of both human creativity and human sin."[37] To change that would be to deconstruct the essence of who we are. His legacy is an indispensable realism based on what he considered to be empirical fact—a fact about human behavior that illuminates the full story of human history and everyone's human experience.

Formulating a doctrine of original sin also requires a definition of sin, and there are many ways to understand our essential sin, such as concupiscence or unnatural desire, pride, egotism, collective egotism, willfulness, wrecked relationships, overreaching, and more contemporary examples such as who will sit on the throne, from the television mega hit "Game of Thrones." The Gospels have very little to say about specific sins but do have a variety of stories that personify sin in some way. The account of the woman accused of adultery in John 8 is graphically depictive. St. Paul writes about the sins of the world in detail and seems to separate sin into three categories of sinning: "God gave them up in the lusts of their *hearts*" to "degrading *passions*" and "a debased *mind*." Sin is such that it corrupts hearts, emotions, and minds. In the three verses where Paul uses the phrase "God gave them up"—Rom 1:24, 1:26, 1:28—he was inferring that God allowed it to happen. But if we begin by asking what is our core or essential nature, then the starting point is not a list of sins but broader categories, such as a divided will, a wellspring of desire, a discontentment with being mere mortals, a history of war, genocide, corruption, rape, etc.

A doctrine of original sin cannot function without reference to a fall of humankind—whether that was a particular moment in time or is a recurring moment in time, whereby we become aware that there is something wrong with us, terribly wrong. Christian theologians ask it this way: what exactly was lost or retained of the *imago Dei* after the fall? Is the effect of original sin such that reason is not only darkened, as Catholics held, but corrupted, as Martin Luther argued. The Roman Catholic Church had good reasons to argue for the former. In baptism, the original taint of original sin is washed away by the blood of Christ. In the sacraments, notably the Eucharist and confession (reconciliation), God's grace is mediated through the Mass and forgiveness. The Protestant Reformers saw this as an overly optimistic position, knowing that the struggle between good and evil is never finished. Even if the sacraments heal and restore, the will, which has been corrupted, falters and betrays us. John Calvin reflects a Reformed theology that concedes something and then takes it away when he writes, "Therefore, even though we grant that God's image was not totally annihilated and destroyed in him, yet it was so corrupted that whatever remains is frightful deformity."[38] This ongoing argument about the gravity of the fall even spilled over into the question of whether all human beings who are living in a state of sin and still retain their free will are able to accept Jesus Christ as their Savior without a born-again experience or regeneration by way of the Holy Spirit. (This too was on the minds of those who gathered and wrote the articles at the Synod of Dort.)

One of the more divisive issues arose when theologians began to write about total depravity, and I find this especially interesting, because it impacts a forthcoming discussion in chapter 4. Consider articles 3 and 4 from the Synod of Dort.[39]

> Article 3: Total Inability
> Therefore, all people are conceived in sin and are born children of wrath, unfit for any *saving good*, inclined to evil, dead in their sins, and slaves to sin. Without the grace of the regenerating Holy Spirit they are neither willing nor able to return to God, to reform their distorted nature, or even to dispose themselves to such reform. (italics added)

> Article 4: The Inadequacy of the Light of Nature
> There is, to be sure, a certain light of nature remaining in all people after the fall, by virtue of which they retain some notions about God, natural things, and the difference between what is moral and immoral, and

demonstrate a certain eagerness for virtue and for good outward behavior. But this light of nature is far from enabling humans to come *to a saving knowledge of God* and conversion to him—so far, in fact, that they do not use it rightly even in matters of nature and society. Instead, in various ways they completely distort this light, whatever its precise character, and suppress it in unrighteousness. In doing so all people render themselves without excuse before God. (italics added)

Article 4 clearly makes a distinction between "the light of nature" whereby we retain some notions about God (the vertical dimension of faith) alongside demonstrating certain virtues (the horizontal dimension of faith) and a *saving* knowledge of God. In other words, our essential nature of goodness persists, but it does not enable us to redeem ourselves.

For the Roman Catholic Church, the Eastern Orthodox Church, and the Reformed Churches (e.g., Lutheran, Presbyterian, Episcopalian, United Church of Christ, Church of the Brethren, Reformed Church of America) this light of nature, this original goodness imparted to all human beings, will flicker but has not been extinguished. In other words, our good self retains the potential of doing good, and it can be inspired to be our best self. But when the context is salvation or conversion, we are not by our own volition or temperament willing to seek forgiveness from God. When we move from the horizontal dimension of loving your neighbor as yourself to the vertical dimension of loving God more than you love yourself, the theology becomes the grace of God, given as gift but never earned.

By shifting our focus from the abstraction of theology to the specifics of a life lived, we gain insight into what matters the most when the question becomes how to live a sanctified life. For Roman Catholics, it is grace mediated through the sacramental life; for mainline Protestant churches, it is Word, sacrament, and Christian education. (The Christian education movement, which is now a given in Protestant churches, was based on the premise that if children were properly educated and nurtured, they would not require a conversion experience.) For Evangelicals and Pentecostals, grace is bestowed when the Holy Spirit touches and moves us.

Philosopher and theologian Nicholas Wolterstorff affirms the Reformed tradtion by stating clearly how he understands original sin. The holistic view of sin and its effects "took the form of resisting all attempts to draw lines between some area of human existence where sin has an effect and some area where it does not." Instead, the Reformers' motivation was to see sin and its effects as leaping over all such boundaries, such that it affects our will as well as our reason. Corresponding to this holistic view of original sin is a holistic understanding of genuine faith. The idea, then, is that "no dimension of life is closed off to the transforming power of the Spirit—since no dimension of life is closed off to the ravages of sin." He concludes: "The scope of divine redemption is not just the saving of lost souls but the renewal of life—and more even than that: the renewal of all creation. Redemption is for flourishing."[40] If you are looking for an even more concise summary of the Reformed theology of original sin, the editor/publisher of the biweekly magazine *The Christian Century*, Peter W. Marty, writes: "My own theological tradition reminds me that each of us is wholly sinful and wholly redeemed, never one without the other."[41]

So what are the truths that endure into the twenty-first century that come to light from a doctrine of original sin?

1. Whatever is wrong with us and whatever we associate with original sin points to an enduring truth that refers to something about us that is universal, enduring, inexorable, and embodied.

2. We cannot grasp our true condition as sinner apart from the gift of redemption, for the gifts of redemption and sanctification include confession, forgiveness, penance, restoration, inclusion in a community of faithful believers where unconditional love is practiced, and living a disciplined life dedicated to serving others, at the expense of putting yourself first.

3. There is something so wrong with us that it deserves the designation of evil, such as genocide, war, torture, racism, child sexual abuse, slavery, caste systems of dehumanization, corporate greed. Evil is not so much the number of dead bodies or the

technical ease by which we now kill, but the way it affects, even transforms, our hearts, our thinking, and our actions. When we sin, we hardly ever deceive ourselves, for we know perfectly well what harm we could cause. But evil is such that it almost always deceives, mostly under the cover of promising something good.

4. In order to comprehend the dismal depth of the human condition, we must give up the precious notion that we can will ourselves to love God and others more than we loves ourselves.

5. Doctrines of original sin and total depravity serve to undercut the presumption that an increase in self-awareness, including education and self-examination, will be sufficient to empower us to do the good we intend. Thus, the distinction between sins and sin, sins being the willful human choices we make and sin being the very core of human nature, so that we have no answer to why I do not love God with all my heart and with all my soul and with all my mind, and my neighbor as myself. (Apropos is this quote attributed to the French philosopher Henri Bergson: "When the self first begins to think of itself, it thinks of itself first.")

6. The theological hypothesis that we are simultaneously sinful and redeemed (*simul est justus et peccator*) is not a contradiction, because human nature evolved so that we exist on the edge of falling toward the good or toward the evil.

7. The fact that we have the capacity for self-transcendence means we are not tethered to the here and now. On the other hand, this very capacity to transcend the present moment means we will also be perpetually discontent with being mere creatures while aspiring to become masters of all that we survey.

RECOMMENDED READING

Fredriksen, Paula. *Sin: The Early History of an Idea*. Princeton, NJ: Princeton University Press, 2012.

Sands, Kathleen M. *Escape From Paradise: Evil and Tragedy in Feminist Theology*. Minneapolis: Fortress, 1994.

Wiley, Tatha. *Original Sin: Origins, Developments, Contemporary Meanings*. New York: Paulist, 2002.

Chapter 4

How Dark Is Dark Enough?

HOW DARK IS DARK enough? I begin this chapter with the premise that this question can be answered adequately only by examining how any religion, Christianity in particular, accounts for sin and not just sin but evil.

Thesis: in its traditional exposition of original sin, Christian theology unduly narrows our understanding of human nature by tilting the balance toward our worst self while neglecting our best self. Traditional interpretations of the doctrine of original sin have also unduly restricted our vision to black and white sins while neglecting the kind of sin associated with systematic dehumanization. With this in mind, we should also be asking if those same traditional interpretations of human nature are dark enough to account for evil so subtle that we cannot name the day or the time when we made a pact with the devil. What should be uppermost in our minds is crafting a holistic understanding that is both bright enough and dark enough to satisfy a theology of original sin and original goodness.

Of all the religious traditions of the world, Christianity has the darkest understanding of human nature. For Judaism, the language of sin is about covenant, about being partners with Yahweh and failing to do so. For Muslims, the fundamental sin is being proud, and for Buddhists, it is investing your life in everything that is actually temporal. With no omnipotent God and no Savior, Hindus "do not believe in sin and so harbor no desire to be saved from it. What needs escaping is not sin but *samsara*" (the vicious cycle of life, death, and rebirth).[42]

Whether from a Christian point of view or not, the question that comes into focus for all of us is when do the dynamics of evil, as distinct from sinful acts, become a focal point in judging how bad we can be when assessing human nature. And this question becomes even more acute as we confront systemic evil, which lies hidden within a promise of some good (e.g., a master race) or when we begin to understand that racism is insidious because it hides within our denial of its existence. The heart of racism, then, is denial and it sounds like this: "I am not a racist."

If you begin with Scripture, most notably the creation account of Gen 1:1–2:4a and the Adam and Eve narrative, there is as much goodness as there is sin and evil. In fact, there is no explicit mention of either sin or evil, but something goes terribly wrong for God to destroy all living things in order to start over. Specifically, "God saw the earth, and behold, it was corrupt; for all flesh had corrupted their way upon the earth" (Gen 6:12). The overall picture does not change when St. Paul addresses the church at Rome. In the first chapter, Paul writes: "So, they are without excuse," which is followed by a declaration that "the judgment of God rightly falls upon those who do such things." They being both pagans and Jews, for every human does evil, "the Jew first and also the Greek," for "all have sinned without the law, and who have sinned under the law" (Rom 1:18—2:29). You know you are up against a very dark understanding of human nature if it requires the sacrifice of the Son of God on a Roman cross.

In St. Paul's understanding of the human condition, humans are ensnared in sins of the flesh and by trying to obey a rigid set of commandments, which in Paul's experience was an unrelenting burden, because the law constantly reminded him of his failure to do what God intended him to do. For Paul, there was no salvation in the law, only the frustration of never doing enough. While this was Paul's experience as a law-abiding Jew, scholars of the Pauline letters find his interpretation of Jewish law to be a misrepresentation of its true intention. For many Jews, even most, the commandments are not a burden but a precious gift that God bestows on Israel to remind them of the reason for their existence. The many dietary prescriptions, likewise, serve to set them apart, because they understand themselves to be the beloved of Yahweh. While Jews are reciting the Shema—"Hear, O Israel! The Lord is our God, the Lord alone"—Catholics are finding a priest to make confession, and Protestants are singing hymns such as "O Sacred Heart, Now Wounded" (st. 2—"What thou, my Lord, hast suffered was all for sinners' gain. / Mine, mine, was the transgression, but thine the deadly pain").[43]

We seem to have neglected that part of the first creation account that laid the groundwork for an original goodness: "And it was so. God saw everything that God had made, and indeed, it was very good" (Gen 1:31). Lest we forget, human beings are equally blessed: "So God created humankind in his image . . . male and female God created them" (Gen 1:27). Historically and traditionally, the doctrine of *imago Dei* had many meanings. Regardless, the new narrative we need to be building is how *imago Dei* includes an original goodness that also defines us. See chapter 5.

Just as we gain perspective when we remove the question of original sin from the context of salvation, we recalibrate our understanding of human nature when a natural goodness has a place alongside original sin. Writing as both a noted author of fiction and a theologian in her own right, Marilynne Robinson strikes the right kind of balance. "The divine image in us, despite all, is an act of God, immune to our sacrilege, apparent in the loveliness that never ceases to shine out in incalculable instances of beauty and love and imagination that make the dire assessment of our character, however solidly grounded in our history and our prospects, radically untrue."[44]

The process of gaining perspective on both how bad we are and how good we can be requires a short review of what has happened since the Reformation. Charles Darwin's theory of evolution laid a number of important theological questions at our feet, and one of the most important is how to think about our distinctiveness. One can point to the divine spark that makes us human, which is a matter of faith; one can point to a moral conscience, which is a matter of observation. What Darwin learned about nature is nothing less than a paradox. Evolution is an amoral process that selects for the fittest with the best chance to survive. Yet he observed that as you follow the ladder that ascends to higher intelligence, you find that both primates and mammals exhibit a sense of empathy, curiosity, and caring for one another, as well as intelligence. Nevertheless, he never departed from his conclusion that "the difference in mind between man and the higher animals, great as it is, is certainly one of degree and not of kind."[45]

Since the publication of Darwin's *Origin of Species* in 1859, great strides have been made to recognize that animals are not only very social, as we are, but self-aware. They are sufficiently self-aware to be able to communicate with each other and with humans. Elephants, for instance, know who their kin are—children, grandchildren, aunts, and uncles—and mourn "loved ones" who have died. Sad to say, they also sense they are being hunted to the point of extinction. Dolphins are trained to follow our hand signals, and killer whales swim aside boats to let us know they are as curious about us as we are about them. This does not mean elephants and dolphins are moral beings, but you can begin to think of original goodness as a process that begins with mammals and primates and ends with human beings. There is much more to add to this picture before we solve the riddle of how an amoral process resulted in a creature burdened with a conscience.

Perhaps no one was more focused on defending Darwin's theory of evolution than Thomas Henry Huxley. But he was among many who misread what Darwin so studiously argued. If you begin where Huxley began, then the doctrine of original sin is your cup of tea.

> The doctrines of predestination, of original sin, of the innate depravity of man and the evil fate of the greater part of the race, of the primacy of Satan in this world, of the essential vileness of matter . . . appear to me to be vastly nearer the truth than the "liberal" popular illusions that babies are born good.[46]

Burning away Huxley's pessimistic depiction of human nature is a mix of contemporary research affirming that humans are born with a natural disposition toward cooperation, which is not learned but develops naturally and is present across a diversity of cultures. Working with a team of researchers at the Max Planck Institute for Evolutionary Anthropology, Michael Tomasello brings to the table a unique combination of decades of experimental work with chimpanzees, bonobos, and human children. What Tomasello learned was the innate ability of children for shared intentionality and cooperation. Present at an early stage of development, rudimentary abilities develop into unique human skills for collective intentionality and the ability to absorb cultural expectations and knowledge for what is acceptable behavior. Finally, by the age of six to seven, children become self-responsible for their own actions.[47]

If any further clarification is needed that humans are hardwired with a sense of morality, it comes from research centers where babies and infants are tested. At the Infant Cognition Center at Yale, for instance, groundbreaking research begins with infants and very young children. Author of *Just Babies: The Origins of Good and Evil*, psychologist Paul Bloom cites numerous research projects confirming an innate sense of morality and helpfulness. Going further, Bloom claims research shows that "certain moral foundations are not acquired through learning," and "they do not come from the mother's knee, or from school or church; they are instead the product of biological evolution."[48] In one typical research project, three-dimensional geometrical objects were manipulated like puppets. In various scenarios, a ball was either helped up a hill or pushed down the hill. The experimenter then placed the helper and the hinderer on a tray to see which one the baby reaches for. "As we predicted," Bloom concludes, "six- and ten-month-old infants overwhelmingly preferred the helpful."[49]

While we rightly make the case for an innate moral sense—which includes a capacity to distinguish between kind and cruel actions, empathy and compassion for others who are suffering, a rudimentary sense of fairness, and a rudimentary sense of justice (a desire to see good actions rewarded and bad actions punished)—our innate goodness is limited.[50] As infants grow to be toddlers, and children transition into adolescence, racial biases emerge, status matters, revenge erupts, and a me-first attitude contends with a natural willingness to help one another. The distinction between what is natural and innate from what is learned and normative represents a basic truth about ourselves that demands remembering.

Finally, we add a dose of evolutionary psychology. Darwin is known for a theory of evolution that is "red in tooth and claw." (That phrase is actually from Alfred, Lord Tennyson's "In Memoriam A.H.H." and predates *The Origin of Species*.) Describing himself as a scientific Calvinist, Huxley understood Darwin to be saying that nature lacks the capacity to produce anything good and so confirms the doctrine of original sin. Our only hope for humanity then is finding ways to curb our natural instincts by means of laws and the enforcement of those laws. That would be to civilize ourselves, which is what we do by way of taboos, rules, and morality.[51]

Huxley's reading of Darwin was misplaced, because Darwin consistently understood evolution to be indifferent. In doing this, he was following the precedent of Enlightenment philosophers, who rejected the presumption that natural evils such as hurricanes were the hand of God as punishment for moral evils. What Darwin denied was the notion of miracle or divine intervention; what he defended was the common origin of all living things. From the very beginning, and gaining strength as he published more books, was his abhorrence of those who were hijacking his science and twisting evolution in order to claim exceptionalism for a particular race. Darwin was even more disturbed by those who advocated for a theory of two different origins for white people and for black people, where the white race is the superior. He was appalled by the economy of slavery, both as England provided ships and America traded in human flesh. His moral compass pointed in just one direction: we are brothers and sisters, one humanity, one tree of lifewith a singular beginning branching in every direction.[52]

Coming to our rescue is Rutger Bregman, and he is confident that we do indeed need to be rescued from our cynicism that is so pervasive it warps our understanding of human nature. Author of *Humankind: A Hopeful History*, he argues quite persuasively that we have been misled to believe that most people cannot be trusted, when in fact we are for the most part decent, kind, and compassionate. If we believe most people can't be trusted, then that's how we treat each other. If we allow ourselves to be drowned in a sea of bad news each day, we will find it difficult to believe that doing good can be contagious, even though we witness it daily and especially when disaster strikes. Immediately after the horrific explosion that rocked Beirut, it was not the government but neighbors organizing themselves to begin a massive clean-up. And during the COVID-19 pandemic, we fed on a feeling that we are in this together and together we will find a way through.

From the many illustrations Bregman provides, two resonate with me. For as long as I can remember, William Golding's *Lord of the Flies* encapsulated the truth about human nature. Regarded as one of our most memorable novels about the end of innocence and the darkness of man's heart, it became an assigned reading for countless young readers. Golding's story begins when a plane crashes on a deserted island, stranding a small group of British schoolboys. The first day, they initiate a democracy of sorts, where everyone has a voice and a job to do. By the last day, when they are rescued by a British warship (symbolic), three are dead, and it had become survival of the fittest. When a ship's officer stands on the beach witness to what he sees, he comments, "I should have thought that a pack of British boys would have been able to put up a better show than this." The story is fictional, yet we read it as a true story. Bregman asserts there is not a shred of evidence that this is what young boys would do if left to their own devices. Bregman in fact uncovered an actual stranding of young boys and learned that they had agreed to work as a team, worked at staying friends, and cooperated to solve problems.

I have also been working my way toward a revised explanation of how modern *Homo sapiens* quickly and thoroughly displaced Neanderthal. Migrating out of Africa around 70,000 years ago from East Africa and overrunning other hominid species in Asia and Europe, *Homo sapiens* established themselves as king of the evolutionary hill. This is known as the replacement theory, and no one doubts that it happened.[53] The debate is about how and why. Noteably in Europe, *Homo sapiens* encountered Neanderthal, a species that had survived two ice ages, were more muscular, had a larger brain, were better adapted to a cold climate, used tools and fire, made clothing, and may have taken care of their sick and infirm. After examining a vast number of Neanderthal bones, anthropologists reached the conclusion that the multiple bone fractures they found were not the consequence of tribal warfare but the courage of an intrepid hunter. The two species were sufficiently compatible to have sex and give birth to children, but only a small amount of their DNA—one to four percent—is found in our present-day genome. So, it could be argued that when confronted with one another, they knew intuitively that this was not going to work out as friends with benefits. Something had to give. In a relatively short period of evolutionary time, Neanderthal became extinct, and *Homo sapiens* lived to write this account. Supported by a growing body of evidence, Bregman believes, as I do, that modern humans did not unleash the first ethnic cleansing but simply outcompeted Neanderthal for the available food and this became possible because we had evolved into an ultimate learning machine, for we were born to learn, to cooperate, and then to trade, share ideas, live together in ever larger communities, and eventually, with the use of language, to pass along valuable know-how that far exceeded learning by imitation.[54]

Surprisingly so, Bregman's brighter view of humanity is playing second fiddle to what is taking place across a much broader sweep of academia. This movement is so pervasive that books keep rolling off the presses with titles such as *The Empathic Civilization* by Jeremy Rifkin, *The Age of Empathy* by Frans de Waal, *The Expanding Circle* [of Empathy] by Peter Singer, *The Rational Optimist* by Matt Ridley, *Abundance: The Future is Better Than You Think* by Peter H. Diamandis and Steven Kotler, and the double-fisted punch by Steven Pinker, *The Better Angels of Our Nature* and *Enlightenment Now*. By marshaling an amazing amount of data, Pinker does a good job of convincing us that the world is getting better in spite of a daily news feed that says otherwise. To follow this line of argument would take a book in itself, but we understand well enough that we live longer, healthier, more secure lives than our grandparents, and we are thankful that we no longer burn heretics as the stake, nor have engaged in a major war since WW II, nor deployed our nuclear missiles, but have found ways to lift millions of people out of subsistent poverty. But if history is to be our teacher, then we need to keep in mind that we remain a self-destructive species like no other.

I trust I have made some points in favor of an original goodness, but any viable understanding of how good we are must include a discussion about how evil changes the discussion of how dark is dark enough. Philosophers and theologians have occupied themselves with reconciling how a good and all-powerful God could create a universe beset with death, decay, plagues, natural disasters, and sinful impulses. Martin Luther reflects a time when evil was personified, as we find in his hymn "A Mighty Fortress Is Our God" ("And though this world, with devils filled, / Should threaten to undo us").[55] Many centuries later, Reinhold Niebuhr writes about evil as a power that antecedes sin (the fall). And there are good reasons to interpret the biblical writer of Genesis as theologizing a talking serpent that simply appears out of nowhere to imply that no one knows the origin of evil, but we surely know it exists.

We do not usually confess our evil intentions, because it is difficult to imagine Christians engaged in the worst of human behavior. Our Sunday morning liturgies are tailormade for sins of commission and omission speaking to a realm of misdeeds and neglect. This is understandable, because evil has a way of blurring our accountability by directing our attention to that one person, a Hitler or a Stalin, who becomes the chief architect of a particular kind of evil. Of course, Auschwitz was the direct consequence of Adolf Hitler and his inner circle of like-minded demigods, but when this is the sole focus of our attention, we forget Solzhenitsyn's warning that to kill by the millions, you need an ideology, and every ideology needs believers. Evil succeeds, because it requires collaborators. It finds them, because it seduces by way of some ideal (a socialist state) and small compromises (giving Eichmann the opportunity to make the trains run on time). Dissecting the anatomy of evil, theologian Miroslav Volf writes: Evil "has colonized us to such a thoroughgoing extent that there seems to be no moral space left within the self in which it could occur to us to hate what we want because it is evil."[56]

Original Sin in the Twenty-First Century

Markus Zusak's *The Book Thief* (now a film) is about a young girl who finds herself living in a small German village where life goes on as usual, even though there is nothing normal about life in the midst of war. Among other graphic scenes, there is one where Jews are being paraded through the streets of the village on their way to Dachau. Everyone turns out to see the spectacle. And everyone understands in some way their fate. Nearly everyone does the easy thing by doing nothing, but one person does the courageous thing. The young girl's father moves out from the crowd to offer a piece of bread to a frail man, barely able to walk. Their reward for providing and for receiving is being whipped by a guard. "Are you hurt, Papa?" she asks. "What was I thinking," he answers, knowing he had just endangered his entire family.[57]

When we think of sin as it is embedded in institutions, corporations, societies, and nations, we begin to understand that evil is not so much the body count, since it creeps along until it has created a toxic culture that in some way dehumanizes others. What happened in Rwanda and Cambodia as the twentieth century ended should not be forgotten. In Cambodia, 1.5 to 2 million people were killed by the Khmer Rouge, and this ethnic cleansing took place as cities were emptied, families broken apart, and the educated targeted for death or exile under the guise of creating a socialist agrarian republic. What happened in Rwanda was a similar process of dehumanization that resulted in the death of 800,000 Tutsi and moderate Hutu in a span of one hundred days; that's 8,000 men, women, and children per day. Sexual violence was so obscene that it is incomprehensible. For the most part, the violence took place at the hands of neighbors and fellow villagers. Leading up to the genocide was a continuous stream of dehumanizing propaganda, principally from a new radio station, and the arming of a selected group with machetes.

Trying to explain this kind of self-destructive behavior is more than difficult. Sigmund Freud tried to explain it by way of a death wish. Acclaimed neuroscientist Antonio Damasio, professor of neuroscience, psychology, and philosophy, and director of the Brain and Creativity Institute at the University of Southern California, Los Angeles, refers to "very old and prehuman biological origins of some of our distinctive behavioral and mental features, a sort of unwashable original sin whose features permeate and corrupt the solutions for human conflict as well as their application."[58] These words are part of the concluding remarks of his book *The Stranger Order of Things*. Overall, he is not very optimistic about our future.

St. Paul, Augustine, Thomas Aquinas, Luther, Calvin—that is, centuries of theological acumen—did not have the contemporary language of *nature vs. nurture* to wrestle with. Augustine was responsible for the dominant Western way of thinking about sexuality. In pondering the Adam and Eve narrative, Augustine fixated on their sexual life before and after their banishment. To be fair to Augustine, he wrote about how concupiscence or disordered desire became our enduring inheritance. In order to explain this, Augustine conjectured that before the fall, if and when Adam and Eve were sexually aroused, there was nothing about which to be ashamed, because disordered desire was not present. But after their denial of God, the ardor of lust became a curse and a touch of evil. Theologically speaking, you might be able to preserve Augustine's identification of original sin with desire, but only in the broader sense that Paul Ricoeur gives it when he writes about a desire that has sprung up "the desire for infinity; but that infinity is not the infinity of reason and happiness . . . but is the infinity of desire itself."[59]

Nevertheless, Augustine's effort to explain an infinity of desire by locating it by way of sexual arousal was destined to become inadequate in an era where sin against God and neighbor manifests itself in so many different ways. Niebuhr, on the other hand, demonstrates an intuitive grasp of a how humans behave in willfully moving between something that is necessary but not inevitable. This theological interpretation of original sin serves to liberate us from a literal reading of Gen 3. A literalistic-historical reading of sin's origin, as Niebuhr argues, undercuts the paradox of inevitability and responsibility, which in turn depends upon a defect in our will to always do the good we intend.[60] There are good reasons to presume that St. Augustine agonized over a book he never finished—*The Literal Meaning of Genesis*—because original sin is something of a paradox, and paradoxes are not meant to be resolved by pondering what kind of sex life Adam and Eve had before the fall.[61]

With the writing of *Emile, or On Education,* Jean-Jacques Rousseau ignited the perennial debate about nature versus nurture, for he argues that children will learn to love just as easily as they will learn to hate, and so begins his manual on parental education with these words: "God makes all things good; man meddles with them until they become evil."[62] Here the doctrine of original sin is abandoned in favor of a theodicy of natural goodness; but be aware that here Rousseau is replacing grace with education. He is also rejecting Augustine's interpretation of the fall as infinite punishment for infinite guilt. Rousseau believed there was no need for theodicy to answer how an all-loving and all-powerful God would permit evil to exist. By taking the responsibility of evil out of God's hands and putting it squarely in ours, Rousseau created a new problem. If evil is our doing in every respect, then surely human beings cannot be perfectly innocent.[63] So whether there is an original goodness or an original perversity in the human heart, as parents, educators, and clergy, we shoulder the responsibility to rear our children to be responsible for their actions, good and bad. So, one vote for the power of nurture. Centuries later, when we have the reality of genes, the voting might as well start over with nature in charge.

When the well-known and well-respected biologist Richard Dawkins published his magnum opus titled *The Selfish Gene,* his purpose was *not* to convince a wider public that such a gene actually exists but to make a more academic argument about how genes are passed along. Such a gene does not exist, though we may wish it did, because it would explain a lot about human behavior. Just as we have learned how interconnected the environmental world is, we have learned that the structure and chemistry of the human brain, intertwined with genes, does not function as isolated systems. But let's consider a different order of things, such as gratitude, humility, reverence, and unconditional love. At best, we might discover a region of the brain that becomes activated, but clearly this is distinct from a life filled with gratitude, humility, reverence, and unconditional love. This is what makes us human, and so the voting must be both nurture and nature.

How Dark Is Dark Enough?

When we try to explain both our good and bad impulses, whether they are innate or learned, it seems to me that we are on much firmer ground if we stick with *willfulness*. Original sin is an enduring truth about our essential nature, because it reveals a truth that everyone experiences in subtle and not so subtle ways. In order for Niebuhr to preserve our situation as one of both finiteness and freedom, he writes: "Sin is natural for man in the sense that it is universal but not in the sense that it is necessary."[64] In other words, a theology of original sin requires us to include the premise that we have evolved in such a way that we are sufficiently self-aware to act willfully and to know that we are doing just that.

What are we to make of the paradox that each of us considers herself or himself to be a good person along with almost everyone else, but still the world is a horrible mess? In order to answer this question, the place to begin is to acknowledge that Christians are not the only moral people in the world. We know that there are enough saints among us who are not Christian to close the door on the exceptionalism of being a Christian. One needs only to consider such familiar names as Thich Nhat Hanh, the Dalai Lama, and Nelson Mandela. The best argument one can make then for the proposition that faith makes a difference is the encouragement and strength that comes from belonging to a community of people who share your values. This observation is grounded in Niebuhr's observation that there is no observable difference between Christians and non-Christians who both do good works except for their motivation, and a sign of that motivation, whether voiced or not, is to be saintly for the glory of God.

Most religious traditions have a high expectation for being a decent and empathetic person who cooperates with others. Muslims stop everything they are doing in order to prostrate themselves before Allah five times a day. Jews religiously keep the Sabbath like no other religion. Buddhism requires a very hard thing: to retrain the mind so that one can live in the moment without any regrets. For Christian believers, the vertical dimension of faith is just as important as the horizontal, thus the great commandment to love God with all your heart, with all your soul, and with all your mind, *and* your neighbor as yourself. In most religions then there is a realism about human nature that pervades its teachings—the road is broad, but the path to salvation is narrow.

So what is missing in this description of religion that answers why the world is filled with so much violence, greed, cruelty, poverty? In part, the explanation lies in the distinction between sin and evil. Religion serves to help us live as good people, caring people, a generous people, and it is here that human nature reflects a common goodness that has the potential to change the world. But as good people, even as faithful Christians, we confess our sins, but we do not know how to confess the evil that thrives on apathy, complicity, indifference, and willful ignorance. At the core of human nature is a self-aware being who cannot transcend an endemic battle of wills between loving unconditionally one moment and in another moment fixating on feelings of jealousy and hatred.

In *Humankind,* Bregman invites us to embrace a new realism. He suggests that "Planet A is where we are kind and helpful human beings and Planet B is where everyone is left to fend for themselves." His new realism is the unspoken truth that "we are living on Planet A, where good people are deeply inclined to be good to one another."[65] In the next chapter I will tell you why I prefer the theological realism of Reinhold Niebuhr, for it takes into account the broader view of history, politics, and of course a wisdom that includes original sin. This chapter has been asking an alternative question: how dark is dark enough? Our worst self is most likely even worse than we want to consider. On the other hand, "each of us is more than the worst thing we've ever done."[66] But also coming into focus is a best self—a self that is more than living a good life. I do hope the officiate at my memorial service (service of thanksgiving), alongside those who knew me best, will have something more to say than "he was a good, decent person." We are capable of more than not messing up too badly. We are capable of more than being kind, friendly, considerate, honorable, nonjudgmental, cooperative, altruistic. We are meant to be redeemed, for all of us are fallen in some way. All of us are called to feed the hungry and thirsty, welcome the stranger, clothe the naked, attend the sick, and visit the imprisoned. All of us are called to love unconditionally—the one who becomes your partner for life, the neighbor next door, the not-like-us person who wants us only to hear his or her story, and every child born to love and to be loved. Every religious tradition seems to understand this, and each tradition has its own particular way to set us on the path of deliverance. If the Christian tradition is distinct in any way, it is so by how it connects the horizontal and vertical dimensions of faith, for when we love God more than self, and when we love our neighbor more than self, the self-loving ego has made space for something better, much better.

RECOMMENDED READING

Bloom, Paul. *Just Babies: The Origins of Good and Evil.* New York: Crown, 2013.

Bregman, Rutger. *Humankind: A Hopeful History.* Translated by Erica Moore and Elizabeth Manton. New York: Little, Brown, 2019.

De Waal, Frans B. M. *The Bonobo and the Atheist: In Search of Humanism among the Primates.* New York: W. W. Norton, 2013.

Neiman, Susan. *Evil in Modern Thought: An Alternative History of Philosophy.* Princeton, NJ: Princeton University Press, 2002.

Tomasello, Michael. *Why We Cooperate.* Cambridge, MA: MIT Press, 2009.

Volf, Miroslav. *Exclusion and Embrace: A Theological Exploration of Identity, Otherness, and Reconciliation.* Nashville: Abingdon, 1996.

Chapter 5

Original Goodness

ORIGINAL GOODNESS DOES NOT enter the stream of theological discourse with a long pedigree of academics waxing eloquently for century after century. There are various reasons for this, but chief among them was the predominance of original sin. This in turn was due to the interlocking nature of sin and redemption and its association with the fall. The sin-redemption narrative was also fortified by St. Paul's influential typology of one man's disobedience and one man's obedience in Rom 5. A secondary reason for the neglect of an original goodness was the way it was subsumed either implicitly or explicitly within the doctrine of *imago Dei* and a theology of original justice.[67] To follow this line of theological thinking, the fall includes in some undefined way original goodness, which is then restored when Christians accept Jesus Christ as their Lord and Savior. But the fundamental culprit for ignoring original goodness is the lack of a clear understanding of what it means in the first place.

What this chapter intends to do then is to give original goodness some distinctive substance. I make no claim to provide us with a definitive understanding of original goodness. My proposal is more modest and will be in three parts: (1) to provide original sin with biblical roots in a way that opens a door to include not only humans but the entire ecosystem of living things; (2) to lead us to discover that original goodness invites a particular way of speaking of the triune God; (3) to enable us to understand original goodness as a counterbalance to original sin; otherwise original sin is a teaching that is inclined to distort a holistic understanding of our essential self.

Anticipating the conclusion of this chapter, my theological argument is this: original sin leads us toward a basic understanding of human nature, while original goodness leads us toward a fundamental truth about all of creation. We know our worst self is one aspect of our essential self. But our best self is an orphan left to defend for itself. Thus the argument that our experience of goodness, beauty, and even grace are gifts of the Creator that we did not bring into existence.

Original sin tells us that there is something terribly wrong with us, and there is nothing we can do about it. Original goodness tells us that there is something beautiful about us, and there is nothing we did to deserve it. Can both statements be true? Or perhaps both are truths that are only fully valid when the truth about human nature is set alongside the truth about the entire creation, for both are created in the image of God.

1. Biblical Roots

When Karl Barth turned his attention to the doctrine of creation (Church Dogmatics III/2), and in particular his theology of what it means to be human, he begins by locating human beings as part of the cosmos (universe). He writes: "In the present exposition we must not and will not be guilty of any failure to appreciate the significance of the cosmos, of any insulating of man from the realm of the non-human creation." And throughout his discourse on "man the creature," he reiterates again and again his concern is to place man within the cosmos and "therefore not with man as alone before God or alone addressed by Him."[68]

In Barth's theology of creation, humans are found in proximity to angels and animals, and we will never truly understand this creature if we forget that heaven is above us and earth below. Thus, if we are to speak of salvation correctly, we should remember the Word of God in its decisive form has a cosmic character, "to the extent that its message of salvation relates to the man who is rooted in the cosmos, who is lost and ruined with the cosmos, and who is found and renewed by his Creator at the heart of the cosmos."[69]

The place to begin our exposition of original goodness is the universe, which is exactly where the first creation account begins. And yet Christian theology has a way of treating the cosmos as a stage where the drama of our personal salvation takes place.[70] In its most restrictive form, the good news is all about God and me, and in its more progressive forms, it is about God and humanity—both as if only human flourishing matters. This excessive anthropocentrism has served to unduly contract God's affirming yes, even though both the Hebraic and Christian Testaments declare otherwise. Thus original goodness cannot be solely about human beings for a number of reasons to follow.

A close reading of Gen 1 reveals that God's blessing includes without distinction plants yielding seed of every kind, trees of every kind bearing fruit, the great sea monsters, every winged bird, creeping things, wild animals, and every living creature. And God blessed them all, saying "be fruitful and multiply and fill the waters in the seas, and let birds multiply" (Gen 1:22). God the Creator also summons humankind, male and female, in the same way: "God blessed them, and God said to them, 'Be fruitful and multiply, and fill the earth'" (Gen 1:28). The gift of creation is life itself, and "life will find a way" (from the movie *Jurassic Park*).[71]

There is though a distinction between creatures of the land, sea, and air and creatures created in the image of God. That distinction is marked with the words "and God said to them." This man and this woman are creatures who can be addressed, who can be summoned to watch over (have dominion over), and be charged with tilling and keeping this good earth (Gen 2:15). Who and what is this human within the cosmos? In his unique style, Barth writes: "Man is the creaturely being which is addressed, called and summoned by God. He is the being among all others of whom we know that God has directly made Himself known to him."[72]

Our unique place in the cosmos is not that of absolute Lord, a second God. Rather, all of life is bound together by the life-giving Spirit that renews the face of the earth: "When you send forth your spirit, they are created; and you renew the face of the ground" (Ps 104:30). Furthermore, nature not only has its own integrity as the dwelling place of God, it reflects the Creator's glory in its own unique way, even without words. Its language is one of terrifying power, stunning beauty, and awe-inspiring complexity.

> The heavens are telling the glory of God,
> and the firmament proclaims his handiwork.
> Day to day pours forth speech,
> and night to night declares knowledge.
> There is no speech, nor are there words;
> their voice is not heard;
> yet their voice goes out through all the earth,
> and their words to the end of the world.
> (Ps 19:1–4; cf. Ps 96:11–13)

In *Ask the Beasts*, Roman Catholic theologian Elizabeth A. Johnson writes: "Individually, we are fellow creatures of the same life-giving God. Together, we are all members of the community of life on Earth. "[73] The reason for asking the beasts is that there is a wildness, an otherness, about them that demands that we respect them for what they are and we are not. We don't mess around with a hungry tiger or a boa constrictor, and we admire them for being not like us. The same can be said for the fury of Mother Nature as she causes the sea to roar and the wind to hurricane. There are moments when the only thing we can do is watch and gasp. The same could also be said for the universe, for it represents its own kind of boundlessness that we are only beginning to understand. The original goodness here is simply everything that leaves us a bit afraid, mystified, awestruck.

The Hebrew Scriptures direct our attention to yet another aspect of the natural world that provokes awe and respect. Consider how Job survives God's interrogation, which begins with a series of questions: Were you there when I laid the foundation of the Earth, or when the morning stars sang together, or when I caused the morning to know its place (Job 38)? God's interrogation is not meant to belittle Job but to enlighten him regarding a world, much less a cosmos, he has taken for granted. Nowhere in Scripture is there such a cascade of mystery and diversity. Job is stunned by the whirlwind of creation's grandeur: the wild ass who turns a deaf ear to its driver, the strength of the wild ox, the ostrich that spreads its plumes aloft, the war horse that laughs at fear, the hawk that soars, the mighty strength of the Behemoth and the Leviathan (Job 39–41). Job is tutored and comes to understand that humans are not the center of everything, and in this way Job is summoned to practice the virtues of humility and gratitude instead of pride and greed.[74] God is the otherness of the cosmos, and in that otherness original goodness is nestled.

Belonging to a community of life means we are bound together in a common redemption. As St. Paul begins his description of our new life in Christ as children of God, he seamlessly includes the creation itself, for it too "will be set free from its bondage to decay and will obtain the freedom of the glory of the children of God" (Rom 8:21). For human beings, the bondage is our willfulness whereby we do what is harmful in spite of our good intentions. For nature, there is no willfulness to be tamed. But decay and extinction are a fate we share: "Not all flesh is alike, but there is one flesh for human beings, another for animals, another for birds, and another for fish" (I Cor 15:39). So what is sown in weakness will be raised to a new glory: "There is one glory of the sun, and another glory of the moon, and another glory of the stars; indeed, star differs from star in glory" (I Cor 15:41). Thus there is reason to believe and to hope that everything that has been created will participate in creation's re-creation, and that is the good news for this community of life.

2. Speaking of the Triune God

One of our most memorable events of the last century was when astronaut Neil Armstrong, placing his left foot on the lunar surface, declared "that's one small step for man, one giant leap for mankind" (July 20, 1969). Millions of us across the globe felt a sense of pride for doing what seemed impossible and a sense of hopefulness about world peace. (Also symbolic of the mission was the decision to leave behind on the moon miniature flags of all nations.) Perhaps not quite as memorable was the picture taken of our planet by the crew of Apollo on its way to the moon on December 7, 1972. The Earth never looked so beautiful, so vulnerable, so isolated, and so special. This image of our planet was quickly given the name the Blue Marble and became one of the most widely distributed images in human history. Unfortunately, we have not yet taken that one giant leap for humankind where the land, sea, and air are cherished as a sacred trust for us to protect.

Eastern Orthodox theologian David Bentley Hart burst onto the theological scene with the publication of *The Beauty of the Infinite: The Aesthetics of Christian Truth*. His book is by no means an easy read, but even if you only grasp a small part of his technical language, the aesthetics of his writing matches the aesthetics of how he understands God. From my perspective, he lays out one continuous argument for original goodness as it is embodied in the Trinity and expressed in the beauty of the creation.

What is foreign about Hart's theology is his resistance to join others who mount a defense of Christian beliefs by appealing to science (empiricism) or to rational arguments that no reasonable person could doubt. The Enlightenment embodied its ideals in statements we are very familiar with: "We hold these truths to be self-evident, that all men are created equal." According to Hart, the two great projects of modernity—the search for comprehensive narratives and establishing an epistemological foundation by way of empirical evidence—were projects that failed to reinvigorate the Christian story of love and peace. Aware of all this as background noise, Hart declares that Christianity has no stake in the myth of disinterested rationality. God's creating does not invite a rhetoric of sound arguments but doxology, hymnody, prayer, gratitude, and a willingness to orient one's will to receive the world as gift. Hart declares that he will not join the search for "how it is" but will direct our attention toward the world "that it is." With this in mind and the declaration that beauty is objective, Hart writes: "There is an overwhelming givenness in the beautiful, and it is discovered in astonishment, in an awareness of something fortuitous, adventitious, essentially indescribable."[75] I ask my reader to keep this quote in mind as we move forward to the third section, where original goodness is a counterweight to original sin, and in particular when we consider what these words mean as we behold the face of a new-born child.

It is very difficult to appreciate Hart's aesthetics of Christian truth by trying to paraphrase him. Hart's rhetoric of beauty seems to come from a different planet, and so I ask the reader to persevere. Thus a sampling of what he writes.

> . . . only if beauty belongs already to the Christian narrative, fully consistently developed, and in such a way as to allay the suspicions it arouses, can the beautiful conceivably meditate the truth without the least shadow of violence.

> Beauty is the beginning and end of all knowledge: really to know anything, one must first love, and having known one must fully delight; only this 'corresponds' to the Trinitarian love and delight that creates.

> Evil is inherently finite . . . when it is exhausted, when all shadow, chaos, hiddenness, and violence have been outstripped by the infinity of God's splendor, beauty, radiance, and delight, God's glory will shine in each creature like the sun in an immaculate mirror, and each soul . . . will turn of itself toward the love of the Trinity.[76]

After reading Hart, there is no way to miss the theme of beauty as it percolates through the opening chapters of Genesis, Psalms, and Job, but we will be tempted to revert back to a reason-based theology. It is telling how often theologians try to convince us of something by appealing to empirical-like arguments. The biblical writers very seldom adopted this approach and clearly did not do so, if we accept the premise that they were making theological arguments first and foremost. Theological arguments about original sin or original goodness are not devoid of factual statements, but they are very seldom pivotal. What matters more is a kind of word truth I emphasized in the first two chapters. Hart begins with the givenness of beauty and argues back to its ultimate origin. He avoids any argument for God's existence based on intelligent design. To go there would be tantamount to acquiescing to the priority of reason.

A much better rhetoric, especially when theologizing about original goodness, is to acknowledge the givenness of creation and the beauty it manifests.

Each of us has her or his own list of beauty as found in the land, the sea, and the air. Limiting ourselves to just two examples of each category, my list includes the tiger and the praying mantis; the star fish and the octopus; any of the seventeen species of macaw parrots and the goldfinch. Each of us has an experience of beauty that is unforgettable. My list of three includes sunset on a beach outside of Athens, a gentle rain as it renews the meadows of Mount Rainier, the moon so close you could almost reach out and touch it. Turning our attention to the human species, both the beauty they are and the beauty they create is astonishing. The body in motion is a beautiful thing to behold: the ballerina; the ski jumper; the body builder; the face that caught my eye, then captured my heart; the expressive fingers that silently convey thoughts and feelings. The beauty we create is limitless: in words, art, music, food, mathematics, etc.

Carl Safina is widely recognized as a bestselling author who knows how to tell good stories—true accounts—about animals. In both *Beyond Words: What Animals Think and Feel* and *Becoming Wild: How Animal Cultures Raise Families, Create Beauty, and Achieve Peace*, Safina demonstrates how scientific research can help us see what we have been missing by presuming we are the superior species (i.e., nothing to learn from a lesser species). With his focus on parrots, macaws in particular, Safina believes he has solved an evolutionary puzzle. Why is there so much beauty in nature, and why do we humans, along with animals, have the capacity to perceive it? In other words, what useful purpose does beauty have in the survival of the fittest? His unconventional conclusion is that beauty is a powerful, fundamental, evolutionary force. This force includes but exceeds the way female macaws choose the most beautiful male, for it happens in many species, including even fish. Furthermore, life has created life so it consistently moves toward both love and beauty. This emotion we call love, Safina writes, "is a feeling telling us we are 'at home' in someone's arms."[77] Of course, that means different things for different species. What we have in common is a feeling of being content and alive here in this place.

As humans, we know what this experience is like in so many ways: watching a beautiful sunrise that completely captures our attention, tiptoeing across a babbling brook (how wonderful is that!), gazing into the midnight sky and marveling at the sheer miracle of the abundance of life here within this immeasurable vastness. Safina's own conclusion is this: "If Life, in its long and difficult journey, has come to be about anything, it is about the progress of love and beauty, the tingle of those Truths."[78]

Now and then, Hart mentions violence as the primary force to threaten beauty. I have in mind the kind of violence that leads to chaos: devastation, disfigurement, rape, torture, genocide, war. Within this the mix of violence is the spectrum of both the natural and human, and they are very different. Violence is violence whenever the givenness of beauty is threatened. The eruption of a volcano is both a beautiful sight but with life-ending consequences. Rape, along with child molestation, only happens when the beauty of innocence is violated. Murder is a sacrilege, because the givenness of life is not regarded as sacred. What every act of violence has in common is when the hand of man despoils the beauty it did not create.

In the twenty-first century, we are aware of violence that threatens to disorder the beauty of the ecological system. Climate change is already unleashing its path of destruction as vast forests burn, rivers run wild from melting ice caps, coral reefs die, once fertile land becomes an arid wasteland, the air we breathe becomes toxic, and the homes of countless species are mindlessly destroyed.[79]

Follow the path of beauty, and it leads to God. Not necessarily so. Alan Lightman, educated as a physicist but better known for his international bestseller *Einstein's Dreams,* begins his *Searching for Stars on an Island in Maine* by relating an experience he had on a moonless night when "my world had dissolved into that star-littered sky" and I found myself sailing into infinity. "A feeling came over me I'd not experienced before" where "I felt a merging with something far larger than myself, a grand and eternal unity, a hint of something absolute."[80] Without engaging in a long discussion of the relationship between science and religion, let's simply keep in mind the difference between a mystical experience and how that is understood from an experience of beauty treasured as the redeeming work of the triune God.

3. A Needed Counterbalance

This book might have been entitled "Original *Goodness* in the Twenty-first Century." I suspect it would not have garnered the same attention, because the Christian narrative from the beginning has been focused on Jesus Christ, Lord and Savior. In the same vein we read John 3:16 for its statement about eternal life, ignoring the first six words, "For God so loved the *world*" (italics added). But even then, we are likely to think of the world as populated exclusively by people who need to be redeemed from their sinful ways. For many reasons, then, original sin has claimed center stage. Yet I found that as my thinking about original sin progressed, something important had been left behind. Original sin needed a counterbalance. It was tempting to rely on the *imago Dei,* because the logic was compelling: if every human being and ever living thing was created to reflect the goodness and beauty of God, then a balance was established. While it is logical to establish an original goodness in God the Redeemer, the consequence is to sacrifice what is distinctive about original goodness; and that would be the enduring truth that divine goodness is imperishable, indestructible, eternally present. There is something reassuring knowing there is a goodness that cannot be taken from us, that endures no matter what, that enlivens creatures of every kind.

My understanding of original goodness is not a figment of my imagination, since it is grounded in three important theological traditions: the Roman Catholic doctrine of natural law, the Protestant understanding of common grace, and the Eastern Orthodox theology of theosis. A very brief summary of each of these theologies is sufficient to clarify where I believe the focus should be.

Natural law appeals to the innate sense of what is naturally good. The universally accepted law that it is morally wrong to kill someone is knowable naturally (intuitively) or by a common use of human reason. Using the same theological interpretation of the natural givens of human life, artificial methods of birth control are not good, because they contradict the natural good of procreation. The sacrament of marriage is good, because it honors the union of a man and a woman who are meant to have children. The crux of natural law then is the presumption that existing alongside a universally accessible moral rationality is an innate sense of what is good and moral.[81]

Protestants and notably Christians of the Reformed faith believe that God's grace extends beyond the salvation of the few. There is then a common grace that is found in beauty, virtue, and excellence in all human beings, including those who do not believe in God. Professor Richard Mouw of Fuller Seminary is well acquainted with John Calvin's effort to honor the difference between special and common grace; the former is associated with predestination and the election of the few, and the latter is coupled with God's providential care that God exercises on behalf of the entire creation. In one of his more forthright conclusions, Mouw argues that since we are now living in a different age from Calvin, we need additional theological resources to promote "conditions for human flourishing."[82] Biblically, Rom 2:14–15 affirms that all humans possess the moral, rational, and motivational resources necessary for doing good things for the right reasons:

> When Gentiles, who do not possess the law, do instinctively what the law requires, these, though not having the law, are a law to themselves. They show that what the law requires is written on their hearts, to which their own conscience also bears witness. . . .

Eastern Orthodoxy has a long history surrounding its distinctive understanding that human beings can have a real union with God and so become like God to the degree that we participate in God's divine nature. This is a theology that presupposes an original goodness as the essence and energy of the Divine that flows through creation, providence, and human beings. While there is no supposition that we share in God's eternal being, the effect of God's transforming grace is such that we live a sanctified life (akin to the process of sanctification). This quote from Macmillan captures the disposition of theosis:[83]

If we let Him—for we can prevent Him, if we choose—
He will make the feeblest and filthiest of us into a god or
goddess, dazzling, radiant, immortal creatures, pulsating
all through with such energy and joy and wisdom and
love as we cannot now imagine, a bright stainless mirror
which reflects back to Him perfectly (though, of course,
on a smaller scale). The process will be long and in parts
very painful; but that is what we are in for. Nothing less.
He meant what he said.

Where my theology differs from these three theological trajectories pertains to a history of identifying original goodness with
human beings. The antidote begins and ends with an original goodness as it is found not just in human beings but in the entire creation,
and not just in the good works of the faithful but demonstrated by
all who are committed to a just society, where none are neglected.
Living in a different age, where our destructive nature warms the
globe unnecessarily, we need to be mindful that we are speaking of
an original goodness that is inherent in the ecological interdepen-
dence of our planet. This biosphere has lasted well over three billion
years and absolutely does not need us, except that it does need us
now to honor a living system that is spectacularly alive.

Who is this stranger standing before me? We have never met
before. She tells me her name, but it isn't a name I can pronounce. As
we become better acquainted and I learn a little of her life's story, I
come to realize we have lived in two very different worlds; hers where
violence was commonplace, mine where it is visualized on television.
I come to understand that if I had not taken the time to ask her name,
I would have thought of her simply as a refugee. And if I had been
a border policeman with a gun, she would have been detained and
asked a fixed number of questions in order to determine who she is.
So often, circumstances do not allow us to take the time to discover
the original goodness standing in front of us, but if we believe that
there is always something uniquely beautiful in what is different from
us, then we will take the time, because it matters greatly.

Born seven pounds, five ounces, he now sleeps secure in his
mother's arms. There is no hint of original sin—how could there
be—and that very thought is an anathema. Though we gladly shared

our genes with him, he will become uniquely his own person. But as adults, we know that our children will learn that not everyone sees the original goodness we see now. Perhaps one day, we will all learn that each of us began life as a child of God, so dearly loved that in the arms of a mother, who loved us unconditionally, tears of joy came streaming down her cheeks.

There is so much about the dirt beneath my feet I do not know. As bread is broken and grace is offered at our table, we give thanks for the good earth, the abundance of sun, rain, soil, the farmers who steward the land. But alas, dirt itself is drying, acidifying, flooding, in ways no human as ever seen before. At the hand of man, dirt itself is being abused by toxic chemicals, overgrazing, and monoculture farming. Left alone, it stores carbon from the air, becomes a home for microbugs who work diligently to turn dirt into fertile humus.[84] And let's not forget that we are soil animals: "And God said, 'Let the earth [dirt] bring forth living creatures of every kind' . . . . And it was so" (Gen 1:24). And so too for human beings, male and female, for they are created from *adama*—living soil or humus. My wife and I have yet to choose our final resting place. It may be a simple rectangular hole in the ground or ashes scatted to the wind. It doesn't really matter, for our life in this world will end the same as every life will end. But God willing, our spirit-souls will join the community of spirit-souls of every kind, and together we will make a joyous sound so beautiful it will please our triune Creator.

RECOMMENDED READING

Hart, David Bentley. *The Beauty of the Infinite: The Aesthetics of Christian Truth*. Grand Rapids: Eerdmans, 2003.

Johnson, Elizbeth A. *Ask the Beasts: Darwin and the God of Love*. London: Bloomsbury, 2014.

Mouw, Richard J. *He Shines in All That's Fair*. Grand Rapids: Eerdmans, 2001.

Porter, Jean. *Natural and Divine Law*. Grand Rapids: Eerdmans, 1999.

Safina, Carl. *Becoming Wild: How Animal Cultures Raise Families, Create Beauty, and Achieve Peace*. New York: Henry Holt, 2020.

Chapter 6

Reinhold Niebuhr—Then and Now

Niebuhr's Serenity Prayer endures more than anything else he wrote, and in a peculiar way, it does define him. Adopted as the official meditation of Alcoholics Anonymous, the prayer begins, "God, grant me the serenity to accept the things I cannot change," then transitions to "the courage to change the things that I can, and the wisdom to know the difference." But when you know even a little more about the person who was an activist, prophet, writer, journalist, educator, theologian, weekly circuit rider preacher, and public thorn in the flesh, you know that Niebuhr had a profound understanding of human nature as it rippled through the tumultuous decades of the Great Depression, two World Wars, the dropping of two atomic bombs, the threat of communism, the Cold War, the war in Vietnam, and the arrogance of American power. You would also know that Niebuhr would have smiled seeing a Black Lives Matter protest sign that read: "I am no longer accepting the things I cannot change. I am changing the things I cannot accept."[85]

Niebuhr did not doubt the power of divine grace to transform human lives, but he rarely spoke of Jesus as repaying the debt of humankind incurred through original sin. While he certainly did not question the reality of original sin, he was prophetic in the sense that our attempt to understand human nature is best done by looking closely at human behavior itself. Niebuhr was neither an optimist nor a pessimist. He thought of himself as a realist with realistic expectations about human beings, even more so when considering the use of power by dictators and presidents.

The publication of his Gifford Lectures, delivered in the spring and fall of 1939, resulted in his seminal theological thinking: *The Nature and Destiny of Man* in two volumes, appearing in 1941 and 1943. The significance of this book is how it became the cornerstone for how he did Christian theology until his death in 1971. Preparation for the Gifford Lectures required Niebuhr to do some serious reading that included Augustine, Kierkegaard, Luther, Calvin, and Emil Brunner's *Man in Revolt*. Certainly pressing on his consciousness was the spread of Nazi tyranny leading to the most terrible example of man's self-destructive nature in human history. So it was no coincidence that Niebuhr brought to the fore an understanding of original sin that included sin and evil, always with an eye on the larger landscape of human history.

As I read him, three interrelated principles encapsulate his understanding of sin and human nature—self-transcendence, freedom, creation in the image of God.

1. All human beings are mortal creatures endowed with the capacity for *self-transcendence*. The former part means all human beings will die, while the latter means we are sufficiently self-aware, being made in the image of God, to transcend the limits of creatureliness. Self-transcendence then is a double-edged sword. It explains our spirituality, that is, our finding our rest in God, offering up prayers and songs of gratitude, and knowing that we are mortal yet hopeful of resurrection. The cutting edge of human life is our incessant desire to overreach, that is, the pride and the will to have more than we need, so that it disturbs the harmony of creation. In other words, we are never content with what is given, with what we have done, and so we reach for the stars and begin evolving ourselves genetically and otherwise. Sin and evil then arise when we falsely believe we can become godlike (the serpent's temptation).

Niebuhr defined our essential self as consisting of two elements. Our essential nature is defined by all our natural endowments, our physical and social impulses, our sexual and racial differentiations—in short, everything imbedded in the natural order. Our essential nature also includes the freedom of our spirit, our capacity to transcend our natural self.[86] What makes the human predicament unique is our belief that we can gradually transcend finite limitations in order to become something we are not at this present moment. We can say with a degree of certainty that no great ape has ever considered transcending the present moment in order to become a better great ape. Only humans find themselves scrutinizing what is past and planning for what could be.

Our creatureliness is good. It is good, because God made us out of love and for love. For Niebuhr, as for Christian tradition, created in the image of God is what defines us as human. But being human means we are not content with being just creature, and thus our undoing is the consequence of believing we are entitled to more and still more. The serpent's temptation was exactly that: "Eve, you are so much more than you think you are." Entering stage left is Hope Jahren, who writes as an environmental scientist and author of *Lab Girl* (2016) and more recently *The Story of More* (2020). [A companion book to Jahren's *The Story of More* is Bill McKibben's *Enough: Staying Human in an Engineered Age* (New York: Henry Holt, 2003).] The story she tells is our history of more people, living longer, spreading out everywhere, increasing our food supply (genetically modified seeds), eating more meat (since 2011, global production of meat has exceeded three hundred millions tons per year), fishing the oceans and aquaculture (more than half the fish now eaten is produced through aquaculture), making everything sweeter (in the 1970s, the average American was ingesting almost one pound of sugar per week, and since then global consumption has nearly tripled), wasting more and using more energy (Americans are the world's heaviest energy users, consuming 15 percent of the world's energy production while making up only 4 percent of the world's population), driving more (one passenger car for every two people of driving age in the United States).

2. Our *freedom* to do the good we intend and the evil we did not intend is both a blessing and a burden. The blessing is the opportunity to be free to explore the universe, create what we imagine, to love another with passion. The burden is one of guilt for what we should have become. What self-transcendence does not grant is a certain path to become everything that God intended us to be. As

Barbara Brown Taylor writes in *Speaking of Sin*: "To measure the full distance between where we are and where God created us to be—to suffer the distance, to name it, to decide not to live quietly with it any longer—that is the moment when we know we are dead [to sin] and begin to decide who we will be tomorrow."[87] One could argue that Adam and Eve were not given the opportunity (freedom) to make things right with their Creator. But they did have the opportunity when "they heard the sound of the Lord God walking in the garden" (Gen 3:8). There was no confession and no request to be forgiven. Instead, they blamed each other and they blamed the serpent.

Niebuhr often speaks of the anxiety that arises when we dedicate ourselves to self-seeking, self-sufficiency, self-mastery, and self-perfection. In his own words: "Anxiety is the internal precondition of sin. It is the inevitable spiritual state of man, standing in the paradoxical situation of freedom and finiteness. The ideal possibility is that faith in the ultimate security of God's love would overcome all immediate insecurities of nature and history."[88] And like many ideals, freedom of choice and freedom of decision are asking for trouble. What actually happens is that our freedom becomes intolerable. In a perfect world and a perfect life, every choice we ever made would be the ideal choice. Reality check: you do remember that we are that kind of creature, one of a kind, where the tragic facts of human history reveal what we would rather not acknowledge? Summing up the connection between freedom and anxiety, Niebuhr writes: "Freedom from anxiety, in other words, is an ultimate possibility, which man as sinner denies in his action."[89]

We are well acquainted with what it means to be anxious. We are anxious about what tomorrow will bring or what the past will not let us forget. Teenagers are anxious about who their friends are and what they are saying about them, continually looking at their smart phones for validation. But when Niebuhr is writing about a fundamental precondition for sin, he is not considering what makes us anxious about tomorrow but with everything that makes us discontented with what we have been given as mortals. The ideal possibility for Christians then is the possibility that "faith in the ultimate security of God's love would overcome all immediate insecurities of nature and history."[90]

Niebuhr also makes another observation that is both theological and empirical. "He [we] can do nothing and regard it perfectly done, because higher possibilities are revealed in each achievement."[91] In other words, we are gifted with unlimited possibilities that we express in the technologies we create and the music we compose, but this gift leaves us anxious, because there is always something left undone, something more to achieve, something about ourselves that isn't quite right. When all is said and done, we could find our rest in the security of God's love, but to do this, we would also need to be content with less.

Old Testament scholar and prophet in his own right, Walter Brueggemann underscores a fundamental disorder that touches every aspect of our lives, one that has become so pervasive we take it to be normative even as we know such unending restlessness is not normative.[92] In *Finally Comes the Poet*, Brueggemann uses the phrase "anxious greed" to identify a fundamental disorder in our lives. The dominant ideology of our culture urges that we must be restless, or we will not get ahead. Appealing to Scripture, Brueggemann has an answer to our disorderly lives. Appealing to two commandments—honoring the Sabbath and do not covet—they converge "in the invitation to yield." Keeping the Sabbath should be the practice of letting life rest safely in God's hand and being content with the gifts given without yearning for more.[93] A second remedy for the restless lives we live is to immerse ourselves in gratitude and doxology, for this is where we become the creatures we are meant to be over against the lives that leave us empty.[94]

A contemporary update is called for. We are indeed anxious and restless about many things. One of the defining features of the technologies of the twenty-first century is how they beguile us with the optimism that anything is possible. Anxiety in today's world is ubiquitous and inescapable. The use of anti-anxiety medications such as Xanax and Valium is so ubiquitous that it is nearly inescapable. Anxiety disorders have become by far the most common psychiatric condition in children, and nearly a third of adolescents ages thirteen to eighteen live anxious lives.[95] There is a lot more happening in the twenty-first century to make all of us anxious: living a meaningful life, a world that feels more dangerous, climate change, and of course a global pandemic. We are even subject to panic attacks, where we are paralyzed. But here the distinction between being anxious and being discontent is important, for only the latter is the precondition for sin. While discontentment begins with a feeling that I can make it right or better, anxiety arises when we doubt ourselves. Discontentment motivates us to work longer hours, climb the highest mountain, discover an ultimate cure for cancer, and even re-make ourselves. Discontentment has energized a very long history of human achievements. On the other hand, anxiety about tomorrow will paralyze us to stay in bed. To clarify then, the precondition of sin is not anxiousness but discontentment, because only the latter leads us to believe we can do better than what Mother Nature has given us.

3. The *image of God* is not destroyed by sin, but it is corrupted. The historical theological debate, notably between Roman Catholics and Protestants, is how deep and how broad is the effect of original sin. Putting aside this debate, we can agree that whether you have never heard the good news, whether you are born again, whether you have yet to repent, our freedom and our willfulness continue to define our essential self. When Christians speak of sanctification—the doctrine that wrestles with what our new life in Christ looks like—they are asserting a new possibility—the possibility not to sin (*posse non peccare)* over against the impossibility not to sin (*non posse non peccare*). St. Paul, and you can include Augustine, affirmed again and again the reality that what grace effects is the unbinding of the human will to overcome evil with good. The biblical witness is unambiguous about the unbinding of the will: the will curved inward to satisfy all things creaturely is transformed into a will united with Christ and the redeeming love of God. The fruits of this conversion of the will are plainly evident: love, joy, peace, patience, kindness, generosity, faithfulness, gentleness, and self-control (Gal 5:22–23).

In describing a sanctified life in Rom 7 and 8, Paul makes a demarcation between then and now:[96]

7:5 *While* we were living in the flesh, our sinful passions, aroused by the law, were at work in our members to bear fruit for death.

7:6 But *now* we are discharged from the law, dead to that which held us captive, so that we are slaves not under the old written code but in the new life of the Spirit.

8:1 There is therefore *now* no condemnation for those who are in Christ Jesus.

8:2 For the law of the Spirit of life in Christ Jesus has set you free from the law of sin and of death. (italics added in above verses)

Outside of this kind of theological language, we must understand that the endemic battle between our best self and our worst self is never entirely resolved. Although the life of the Christian takes place in the context of the lingering of the old age, our new life in Christ is no longer in bondage to the infectious power of sin. Yet we know others who demonstrate the fruits of conversion, who are not Christians. Nelson Mandela's story is that of someone who was reborn, and this took place while serving twenty-seven years in prison for treason against the government. He could have emerged from prison as a defeated, angry, revengeful shadow of himself. But somehow from the books he read, the continual stream of correspondence with loved ones and comrades, the fellowship of fellow prisoners, the small pots of plants he tended, the conversations with guards, and his will to live to see his beloved country governed by all the people, Mandela stood tall and proud, willing to compromise with those who ruled as white supremacists, but always from a position of dignity and fairness. So I reiterate that the one claim Christians can make for themselves as sanctified sinners is a heart that is full of gratitude, ready to sing a joyous song (such as "Morning Has Broken"—you name your favorite hymn of praise and gratitude).

Racism is demonic for the way it coyly infers that not everyone is made in the image of God. So why haven't white Christians, male and female, been forthright and visible in the Black Lives Matter movement of 2020? The obvious reason is our difficulty to see the image of God in others, because we have been born into a worldview where privilege is taken for granted as a birthright. Racism in America is also an economic story, where the disparities in income, health, and education should be an outrage. (According to the Brookings Institution, the average white family has a net worth that is nearly ten times as great as that of the average Black family.[97]) I am aware, as you are, that this is not the kind of discussion Calvin and Luther had when writing about a corrupted *imago Dei,* even though economic disparity was probably as acute then as it is now. And what would they have said about the present Black Lives Matter movement? In fact, we have some idea, because Luther was initially supportive of a nonviolent revolt from below (peasants) but then sided with the burghers, the nobility, and the princes when it turned violent. Theologically speaking, Luther was not thinking of himself as part of a caste system willed by God, supported by clergy, and confirmed in Scripture, but that was exactly what was taking place. (Here I am looking ahead to chapter 7, where Isabel Wilkerson clarifies the role of caste systems intended to maintain a system of hierarchy in order to sustain one's own ranking, advantage, and privilege.) If that is so, then being made right with God (sanctification) includes joining the Wall of Mothers as those who understand how it feels to be systemically dehumanized.

After reading Isabel Wilkerson's *Caste: The Origins of Our Discontents,* I have another response to how we can be a good person among a world filled with good people and still live in a world where dehumanization is another stain on our record of being human. Caste systems have been in place for hundreds of years, even thousands, for the sole purpose of subjugation: the Jews in Germany, African Americans in the United States, and the untouchables in India. (There are many more examples, but these three are highlighted by Wilkerson.) Pulitzer prize winner and reporter for the *New York Times,* Wilkerson explores eight pillars that underlie caste systems across civilizations. Taken individually and together, these pillars create their own self-serving worldview: divine will and the law of nature, heritability, endogamy and the control of marriage and mating, purity and pollution, occupational hierarchy, dehumanization and stigma, terror as enforcement and cruelty as a means of control, inherent superiority versus inherent inferiority. As a self-identified white person, I felt demoralized by what I learned at the level of asking myself how we could have allowed this to happen. While I did not have a direct hand in the establishment of any of these pillars, I can understand at another level how I have been part of a worldview where white privilege is the norm, a worldview that I am morally obligated to cross-examine.

Niebuhr's realism—Niebuhr's political realism is rooted in his methodological commitment to the obvious facts (the truth) of human nature. Instead of defending a particular doctrine, he persuades by asking you to pay attention to human history. When it comes to preaching the gospel, Niebuhr prefers to wrestle with the messy reality of the will-to-power, the irony of history, and the enigma of a species that fails again and again to achieve the good it intends. When he speaks of the children of light, Niebuhr has in mind both liberal and conservative Christians who participate in the sin of a moralistic Christianity, namely, "The greatest sin of moralistic Christianity is its tendency to encourage the assumption that men are as good as the ideals of justice and love which they entertain."[98]

Niebuhr had no systematic theology on which to invoke. Nevertheless, when his attention turned to a long look at history, he reminded us that original sin explains why the highest human achievements are infected with corruption. It is here that you begin to understand that ideals are dangerous in so far as all historical configurations of power are a mixture of good and evil.

Both Jimmy Carter and Barack Obama referred to Reinhold Niebuhr as their favorite theologian. The same is also true for Arthur Schlesinger, John McCain, and the *New York Times* reporters David Brooks and Ross Douthat. President Cater may have misunderstood him, but Obama did not. For Carter, Christian ideals and Christian ethics were a sufficient guide to being a good person and a good president. Perhaps forgetting what he owed to Niebuhr, Carter saw himself as a moral leader of a moral nation. While Carter and Obama shared a common hope that Christianity could be a force for justice in the world, only Obama struggled mightily to craft a foreign policy that took into account that it is simply impossible to translate Christian personal virtues into the larger, impersonal scale of foreign policy.

Niebuhr's realism is proving to be more valuable in the twenty-first century than the twentieth, though the long perspective was the source of his authority. Beginning with the premise that no use of power is fully innocent and that every political decision involves the sacrifice of one value or another, as Niebuhr did, then the decision-making process of a president is always ambiguous. Thus Obama's reluctance to use American air power to save untold human lives in Syria, even after he had learned its leaders had use chemical weapons on its own people. Thus our after-the-fact awakening that led us to the verdict that the war in Vietnam was predicated on a pack of lies. Thus only after we had bombed the hell out of Iraq did we begin to acknowledge the self-serving idealism that we could rebuild the country in our image. Thus our engagement in an endless war in Afghanistan based upon the presumption that their soldiers and their elected leaders would be sufficiently motivated to fight the good fight. Let's just say there is something unnatural and very difficult for power submitting to self-criticism through understanding one's past. What was neglected then and now is Niebuhr's long historical perspective that leads to the wisdom that history cannot be coerced.

Niebuhr defied the usual labels of conservative, evangelical, radical, or even liberal. In today's world, where political divisions are everywhere, Niebuhr would have found President Trump to be superficial for a reason not usually considered, namely, Trump didn't agonize over important decisions that affected the lives of millions. This same critique applies to those who hold onto religious convictions that turn agonizing decisions into black and white certainties, but hopefully not quite in the same dramatic way as Trump exemplified. Niebuhr was a thorn in the flesh, for in both his writing and preaching, he spared no one. That thorn is how the curious mix of good and evil reflects the inexhaustible schemes of humans and nations. There were occasions when Niebuhr was criticized for a theology that led to indeciveness that turns into non-action. Then again he was criticized for defending the rightness of civil disobedience. But Niebuhr held to his conviction about the illusion of idealism—"the idealism of noninterventionists, who are embarrassed by power, and the idealism of imperialists, who disguise power as virtue."[99] These are the words of David Brooks when referring to Niebuhr's realism as a form of humble hawkishness. And the context for this deliberation was George Bush's war on terrorists after 9/11.

In writing about American history, Niebuhr wanted us to understand how many of our idealistic endeavors as a nation were cruelly refuted by reality. Many of those ironic outcomes resulted from the false perception of our exceptionalism, ranging from the self-made autonomous individual to the delusion of omnipotence leading to endless wars of liberation.[100]

One does not usually think of Barack Obama as the war president, but just ruminate on these places and names during his two terms: Iraq, Afghanistan, Libya, Syria, Egypt, Ukraine/Russia, Taliban, Muammar Gaddafi, Osama bin Laden, ISIS, Bengasi, chemical weapons, Armenians (again), Arab Spring. In *The World As It Is: A Memoir of the Obama White House,* Ben Rhodes, the president's speech writer and confidant, chronicles each crisis as it unfolded. It was fortuitous that Obama was awarded the Nobel Peace Prize as he began his first term, for it is difficult to think of another president who was continuously confronted by the agonizing decisions whether to intervene or not. Those decisions are made excruciatingly difficult when you are the richest and most powerful nation in the world. The lesson learned by Obama, as reported by Rhodes, was to balance the truth of the world *as it is* (the realist) and the world *as it ought to be* (the idealist).

Reading Samantha Power's memoir, *The Education of an Idealist,* you are again drawn into the conscience-wrenching decisions Obama had to make as president. Power writes from the vantage point of being a war correspondent and well acquainted with evil as it unfolded in Bosnia. That experience became a Pulitzer Prize-winning book that registered her indignation over our failure to intervene—*A Problem From Hell: America and the Age of Genocide.*[101] Her career took a radical turn from outsider to insider when she was appointed special assistant to President Obama and then the United States ambassador to the United Nations (2009–2013). In both of these positions, she demonstrated her passion to advocate for human rights as an essential part of what our country stood for. When considering Power's tenacity, Rhodes remarks that she was the one person he most wanted to become when he moved to Washington, because she supported an interventionist America that promoted human rights, and yet she opposed the war in Iraq, "standing apart from many liberal interventionists who were co-opted by the Bush crowd."[102]

Power begins her own memoir this way: "Some may interpret this book's title as suggesting that I began with lofty dreams about how one person could make a difference, only to be 'educated' by the brutish forces that I encountered. That is not the story that follows." So what is her story as one who participated in the decision-making processes of Obama? Her education did include "to better appreciate the constraints that stand in the way of making positive change" and to remember Niebuhr's words of wisdom that "we must always seek the truth in our opponent's error and the error in our own truth." But the final words of her book are more personal. After recalling her relief when hearing of a father who had been reunited with his son, newly free of a deadly disease, "I came to the conclusion that people who care, act, and refuse to give up may not change *the* world, but they can change many individual worlds."[103] It would seem that Samantha Power remained an idealist, but a wiser one.

Quotes too good to omit:

- "The final enigma of history is therefore not how the righteous will gain victory over the unrighteous, but how the evil in every good and the unrighteousness in the righteous is to be overcome."[104]

- "Man's capacity for justice makes democracy possible; but man's inclination to injustice makes democracy necessary."[105]

- "Thus some evil, which is to be destroyed, is always transferred to the instrument of its destruction and thereby perpetuated."[106]

- "The gospel cannot be preached with truth and power if it does not challenge the pretension and pride, not only of individuals but of nations, cultures, civilizations, economic and political systems."[107]

- "To love our enemies cannot mean that we must connive with their injustice."[108]

- In jail in Birmingham, Alabama, in 1963, Martin Luther King Jr. drew on this passage from memory in his open letter to eight of the city's white clergymen. "As Reinhold Niebuhr has reminded us, groups tend to be more immoral than individuals. We know through painful experience that freedom is never voluntarily given by the oppressor, it must be demanded by the oppressed."[109]

RECOMMENDED READING

Brueggemann, Walter. *Finally Comes the Poet: Daring Speech for Proclamation.* Minneapolis: Fortress, 1989.

Ellie, Paul. "A Man for all Reasons." *Atlantic*, Nov. 2007. https://www.theatlantic.com/magazine/archive/2007/11/a-man-for-all-reasons/306337.

Gilkey, Langdon. *On Niebuhr: A Theological Study.* Chicago: University of Chicago Press, 2001.

Power, Samantha. *The Education of an Idealist: A Memoir.* New York: Dey Street/William Morrow, 2020.

Rice, Daniel R., ed. *Reinhold Niebuhr: Revisited.* Grand Rapids: Eerdmans, 2009.

Chapter 7

The Challenge of the Twenty-First Century

IF ANYONE ASKS YOU what this book is about, you will tell them it is about these two words. These two words should be tweeted and posted and let loose across the globe. Anyone with imagination should make a TikTok video so we can visualize them. Designers and manufactures should use their creative skills to emblazon handbags and watchbands with them. With their history of good intentions, Starbucks should imprint them on every coffee cup sold across the world. On billboards, and especially incorporated into every stop sign, let them be a constant reminder. Let us not forget the doorways of classrooms and laboratories, where students learn the essentials of what they need to know in order to succeed.[110] And what are these two words: **BE VILIGANT.**

The summer of 2020 taught us what it means to be vigilant. Then as the number of deaths from COVID-19 went down, then went up, then went down, we learned to be vigilant or suffer the consequences. We learned the hard way that being vigilant is important. The challenges of the twenty-first century present an array of trajectories, and what they have in common is the way human beings find themselves at the fulcrum of how we fare as a species.

We are living in an era where the human hand is everywhere. Let me begin with a very, very short history of our evolution as a species in order to contextualize our present predicament. From the beginning, we felt a sense of discontentment with living in trees, and so we climbed down in order to explore, conquer, and remake our world. We never settled in just one place. We never felt fulfilled with our lives as they were. We were satisfied with a club until we realized the potency of a spear, then a bow and arrow, then a gun, succeeded by the atomic bomb. First we walked, then we ran, then we rode, then we motorized, then we flew, then we began to go where no one has gone before. Our footprint, though, was never pretty, and yet as we began to judge Mother Nature to be unnecessarily cruel, we began building hospitals and providing year-round training for 7,000 athletes from 170 countries under the umbrella of Special Olympics. If this is who we are, coupled with a heightened sensitivity to right and wrong, it almost explains everything about human nature, while leaving us to ponder if we were destined from the beginning to transcend instinctual behaviors that no longer serve us well.

To use broad strokes again, the term Anthropocene (the age of humanbBeings) is no longer just an academic designation but a description of a new reality where the hand of man is everywhere, while the hand of God is melting away.[111] The hand of man is my shorthand for our incessant drive to remake everything to suit our needs and our desires. Our need to eat and survive and even flourish is understandable. What is disappointing and even alarming is our overreaching in the sense that we will edit the genes of our unborn children to meet some cultural standard, such as gender, height, intelligence, body shape—and we will do this as an expression of our desires rather than for the good of all. In direct opposition, the hand of God is my way of referring to the mystery of the divine presence as it pulls creation toward its appointed place, as it guides and calls us to be better than we thought we could be (saints), creates human beings with hearts capable of unconditional love, and infuses all living things, even matter, with an energy that is inexplicable and ineffable.

We are living in an era where the human hand is everywhere, but what exactly does that mean? Let me count the ways (well, just a few). The food we eat, of course. Did you know there is a billion dollar race to cultivate a burger in a lab by culturing cells, such as hardy fungus and muscle tissue? Those leading the way hope to cash in on the summons to lower our carbon footprint by not killing a single animal. This is sometimes known as the Billion Dollar Burger because this may be the food of the future.[112] (Burger King has been selling a meatless Impossible Whopper since 2016.) When we do slaughter cattle for the hamburgers we eat, they are most likely eating corn that has been genetically modified, and their natural cycle of eating and living has been modified in multiple ways toward the singular end of a one-thousand-pound steer in the shortest time. Lactose-free milk? You can find it in the supermarket through a process of breaking down the complex lactose disaccharide into two simple sugars. We have come a long way from just naming the animals (Gen 2:20).

What is more natural than giving birth to your firstborn child? Not quite natural: this infant in your arms became a reality because you froze an egg years ago, and the egg was then fertilized in a petri dish. Then you followed the advice from the Jewish Genetic Disease Consortium that "all couples with any Jewish ancestry, including interfaith couples, should have pre-conception carrier screening for all Jewish diseases." Finally your son (your ultrasound confirmed your intuition) was delivered by cesarean section. (More than one third of U.S. babies and more than 40 percent of Chinese babies are delivered in this way.) If you live in the state of Massachusetts, your newborn was screened for fifty-two genetic disorders.[113] And by the way, you met the love of your life on a dating app, then compared your genetic suitability by way of 23andMe.

Consider the following real-life dilemma. She was pregnant with twins after six years of fertility pills, ovulation injections, donor eggs, and disappointment; but reproductive medicine had now set up a choice that made her very uncomfortable. The idea of managing two infants at this point in her life terrified her. Jenny and her husband already had grade-school children and limited resources, and twins felt like an all-consuming and out of control situation. Yet the thought of not having one of them also felt unbearable. Jenny reflected: "If I had conceived these twins naturally, I wouldn't have reduced this pregnancy, because you feel like if there's a natural order, then you don't want to disturb it. But we created this child in such an artificial manner—in a test tube, choosing an egg donor, having an embryo placed in me—and somehow, making a decision about how many to carry seemed to be just another choice. The pregnancy was all so consumerish to begin with, and this became yet another thing we could control."[114]

Welcome to the twenty-first century, where technology outpaces cultural consensus and plunges the individual into the position of making godlike decisions. Regardless of how you judge Jenny's decision—whether she crossed the line between a procedure done for medical reasons or for personal reasons—we will be compelled, increasingly so, to make ethical decisions in matters of life and death. Those kinds of decisions are very different from those focused on climate change or re-engineering our bodies in order to escape genetic diseases and prolong the average lifespan. First we must acknowledge that when we escalate the pivotal role we play, when we create technologies meant to enhance us in some way, it is human nature that comes to the forefront, because to be human is to project ourselves into everything we do. Thus, identifying and clarifying what is our essential self is where we need to start.

Is the day coming when all or most of us will be living with modified genes, modified by human intervention rather than random selection? At some point in our history, evolution produced an enhancement endowing us with the ability to create a self beyond what nature gives us. The driving motivation behind this Huxley-like future will not be government, not public consensus, and not science. Ultimately, human instinct will assert itself, and mothers and fathers will do the most natural thing they can do—help their children achieve health, happiness, and success. By believing they are the best parents they can be, they will be making choices that reflect the values they hold most dear. Those values given to us by place and time, by culture and ancestry, are most likely ones we have not examined with a eye toward a future when technology imposes on us a new question: who do we want to become? This is the kind of question our ancestors did not have the obligation to ask.

The Danish experiment, as I choose to call it, unfolded when Denmark offered free prenatal Down syndrome screening to every pregnant woman. This was in 2004. Since then, the annual number of babies born to parents who chose to continue pregnancy after a prenatal diagnosis has ranged from zero to thirteen. With this in mind, we understand why Down syndrome is frequently referred to as the canary in the coal mine for selective reproduction. What is interesting is the reasoning that goes on when parents make the decision to abort or not. Writing a story for *The Atlantic*, Sara Zhang interviewed a number of mothers living in Denmark. Their decision to abort was always agonizing, To give birth to a child is to commit yourself to unconditional love for a lifetime. Down syndrome complicates the decision-making process, because there is a possibility your child could have a wide range of severe intellectual disabilities and physical ailments. But overall, the primary characteristic of this genetic malfunction (an extra copy of chromosome 21) is an individual who responds to whatever life brings in a nonjudgmental and open way. The primary reason then to abort seems to be the uncertainty of the unknown, and along with that uncertainty comes the realization that nature is not cooperating by guaranteeing a perfect child destined for high achievements. The Danish experiment is having its own unintended consequence. Women realized they were not the mothers they thought they were—the kind who "chose to not have a child with a disability."[115]

As genetic testing becomes widespread and readily available, the broader question posed by a genetic counselor at Sarah Lawrence College is this: "If our world didn't have people with special needs and these vulnerabilities, would we be missing a part of our humanity?"[116] Everyone who lives in a privileged society knows it is not easy to give up the dream of a perfect child, for that is what we are learning to expect; but Mother Nature stands in the way. When a medical system is dedicated to giving parents the tools to decide what kind of children to have, then giving birth to a child becomes a litmus text for what we value most about human love.[117]

So we begin the era of evolving ourselves. Informing us about what to expect, Juan Enriquez and Steve Gullans instruct us to learn two terms: *unnatural selection* and *non-random mutation*. Enriquez served on the Genetics Advisory Council at Harvard Medical School, and Gullans has published more than 130 scientific papers in leading journals. Together they are the authors of *Evolving*

Ourselves and cofounders of Excel Venture Management, which enables start-ups in synthetic biology and new genetic technologies. Our future, as they argue, will be our moment in history to overthrow Mother Nature by developing the knowledge to re-engineer genes, so we are no longer at the mercy of mutations that may or may not be good for us. And why will we do this? Because we can! As Enriquez and Gullans remind us, our laws, our moral codes, and our institutions were built to fulfill the ideal that we care about every child that is born, including the most diverse and vulnerable.[118]

I am confident that most of us are in agreement that survival of the fittest is no longer the way we want to envision the future. Yet, once we invite into our lives an original arrogance that whispers in our ear "we really need to do this and to do it now," we have opened the door to another kind of future, where everything depends upon the hand of man. Once again, we bump up against Niebuhr the prophet telling us that "no use of power is entirely innocent." The kind of power we wield in the twenty-first century is subtle, ubiquitous, and infused with optimism, promising a better future.

Should we be worried or concerned when science moves faster than the public debate about how much and how fast? Yes. But be mindful that, for the most part, the scientific community is well aware of what could go wrong. Michael Bess, professor of history at Vanderbilt University, covers the basics in *Our Grandchildren Redesigned:*[119]

- An inevitable disruption of the normal cycle of an older generation giving way to a younger generation.

- When we are able to modify the genes of our yet to be born children according to our desires, are we failing to appreciate our children as gifts not of our own doing, favoring hubris over humility?

- A growing rift between the biologically enhanced and those who can't afford it.

- A constant cycle of upgrades that never leaves you satisfied, especially if you are expecting perfection and living to be 125 (or is 150).

- The risk of disrupting the core set of values that inspire our better self.

The debate that takes place among scientists is not only what might happen if we do this or that. The debate also takes place when we fail to take full advantage of innovations with the potential to save lives, and not only to save lives but to rid the world of devastating diseases and viruses. If one dimension of sin is to overreach, the other dimension is to allow caution and fear to impede meaningful progress.

If only Eve and Adam had been vigilant, they would have been suspicious of a serpent that promised them an infinity of possibilities. That isn't the way the story is told, because the biblical narrator understood our true disposition.

> *Prayer*—O Lord, we confess that there are times when we do not care about what we want to become, as an individual, as parents, as a congregation, as a nation. The measuring rod is of course unconditional love. So let this be our prayer as we choose the values that will guide our lives.

Is it a sin to frack for oil and gas? Is it a sin when fracking enables us to become an energy independent nation? When fracking creates a wealth of new jobs? To be more specific, is fracking a sin because of *passivity and indifference*? For the first time in our history, our beautiful, life-giving planet, in its entirety, has become an urgent concern, because, formerly, we had better things to do with our time and money. The question about fracking does not exist in isolation from global warming and those most affected by climate change. While both primitive and traditional religions have honored Mother Earth and even deified her in some way, fracking is different, because we are beginning to realize that we are both the problem and the solution.

The Challenge of the Twenty-First Century

If there is sin to be named, where does the ax fall? The farmer who sold or rented his land to an oil or gas company? The consumer who, even though the miles per gallon is posted on every new car sold, continues to buy a two-ton SUV, having no second thoughts whatsoever? (A 2021 Toyota SUV weighs 3,761 lbs.) The corporate executives and their board of directors who are aware of the science of global warming but continue to frack until it becomes unprofitable?

Who is my neighbor? When measuring the impact of global warming, the entire country of Bangladesh is my neighbor. So are the certain to come wave after wave of climate migrants. (Driven by food insecurity that is driven by climate change, the total global migration estimates range from 50 million to 300 million. In the northern part of South Africa, droughts have already killed 100,000 people.[120]) Is our empathy and our Christian faith sturdy enough to do unto others as we would have done for us? The judgment scene in Matt 25 needs a twenty-first-century addition. When all the nations are gathered before the Son of Man, they may be asked, when did we see you a refugee with no land to farm and no water for irrigation (Matt. 25:31–46). And we will say to Christ the Redeemer . . . ?

The question about fracking then draws us into an era where we need to examine sins of passivity and indifference. To be forewarned is to be forearmed, and in this instance by doing next to nothing of any consequence, we have done something quite awful. Most of us do not see it that way, because we are so focused on the immediate that we are indifferent, apart from what affects us in the immediacy of a few years. Global warming is not like any other moral issue we have known, because it demands that we care about a future that is thirty years long (2050), a population that is too easily villified (millions of climate migrants), and the extinction of multiple species about which we know too little to understand how important they are to maintaining a healthy ecosystem. For the few who regard climate change as a crisis demanding our immediate action, there are the many who are doggedly reluctant to change both their values and their habits. Here the sins of passivity and indifference translate into the proactive sin of destroying the ecosystem of our beautiful, blue-green home.

Original Sin in the Twenty-First Century

Prayer—O Creator of the universe, forgive us for choosing to be indifferent about the fate of this absolutely awesome, life-sustaining, one of a kind—as far as we know—home. Amen.

St. Paul may not have been the first to use the phrase "the good fight" (2 Tim 4:7), but it is clearly apropos for very different reasons in a century where our resolve will be tested. By now, almost everyone has heard of the goal of net-zero emission by 2050. (Net-zero refers to a goal where certain exceptions are made, such as the fuel used to fly airplanes, but only when they are offset in some way; the aerospace industry could fund hundreds of wind farms.) There is no way we will reach that goal if big oil and big gas are allowed to operate as usual. In what sounds like a repeat of misinformation spread by big tobacco and big agriculture-chemical conglomerates like DuPont, big oil continues to fund lobbyists to weaken policies that would hasten a shift to clean energy. As Christians, we have a responsibility to be faithful stewards of God's provision, but this now means taking on the big boys. When it comes to taking on the big boys, two names stand out. Bill McKibben is best known for building 350.org, the first global citizens movement to combat global warming. He has also been in the forefront urging universities, nonprofit organizations including churches, and for-profit corporations to take their money out of dirty fuels and reinvest it in green energy.

With her book, *The (Burning) Case for a Green New Deal*, Naomi Klein may sound like a radical, but she understands herself to be a realist. The realist understands that the core of our economic system and our planetary system are now at war with each other, and only a bold program such as the Green New Deal can meet the challenge of changing everything. The good fight Klein wants us to understand does not depend on what I can do as an individual. "In fact," she writes, "the very idea that we, as atomized individuals, even lots of atomized individuals, could play a significant part in stabilizing the planet's climate system or changing the global economy is objectively nuts."[121] The same should be argued about the adequacy of being good stewards of the Earth. The good fight in this instance, and in any instance where an original sin is manifested in deep-seated structures of inequality and degradation, is to be part of a massive and organized global movement. Our mandate from God is not in question, but this is not the same Earth as it was when Scripture was written. Like the mandate to go forth and multiply, our mandate to steward the earth has shifted. Over our relatively short history of mining the earth for all it is worth, and an even shorter history of the Industrial Revolution, we have plundered, ravaged, depleted, despoiled, and polluted the land, sea, and the air we breathe while endangering all living things. Tending and conserving are simply inadequate, because we need to be building a new energy infrastructure in order to heal Mother Earth. Waiting patiently for big oil, big gas, and big coal to leave assets in the ground is childish. And can we now say sinful?

To grow up and act responsibly is to learn from the past, and part of that past is the road that led to passing the Nineteenth Amendment to the Constitution. For more than half a century, women of this country, both radicals and slow but steady workers, persevered until a single vote in the Tennessee House of Representatives ratified the Nineteenth Amendment. Even then that single deciding vote was the result of a mother's letter to her son, Harry T. Burn, telling him "don't forget to be a good boy." But don't believe for a moment that this fight was over. Almost immediately, opponents of the Nineteenth Amendment tried to discredit the legitimacy of the ratification by accusing Burn of taking a bribe. Next, they manufactured witnesses and affidavits intended to smear Burn if he did not recant his vote. Burn never recanted, but opponents continued until every last-ditch effort failed, including an appeal to the Supreme Court.[122]

The lesson we cannot forget is best captured in the tag line from Ken Burns's documentary about women suffragettes: "No one gave us anything. We took it."[123] The Nineteenth Amendment should have included African American women, Asian American women, Hispanic American women, Native American women. It did not, because various structures of discrimination remained in place, requiring another good fight that included the repeal of the Chinese Exclusion Act in 1943, the adoption of the Immigration and Nationality Act of 1952, the Twenty-Fourth Amendment in 1964, and the Voting Rights Act in 1965, culminating in the Equal Rights Amendment of 1972, which would have granted legal equality regardless of sex. (The Equal Rights Amendment was ratified by the required number of thirty-eight states but is still not formally ratified unless the Senate votes to backdate the deadline for states to ratify.)

The Civil Rights Act of 1964 prohibiting discrimination in public places, including schools, is yet another good fight that became a long fight, achieved by the lives of innocent children in the ashes of the Sixteenth Street Baptist Church (1963) and Bloody Sunday at the Edmund Pettus Bridge, Alabama, where protest marchers were met with horses, billy clubs, and tear gas (1965).

> *Prayer*—Eternal God, forgive us when we do not join the
> good fight that requires a lifelong commitment, knowing
> full well that the next generation will have its own good
> fight to take up. Amen.

Are white privilege and white fragility *sins of complicity*? Toni Morrison has identified white racism as one of distraction, a device that "keeps you explaining, over and over again, your reason for being."[124] In other words, racism is so well hidden within the presumptions of white culture that it never rises to the level of consciousness where it can be examined, and if examined, then to the level where one becomes accountable. The way those presumptions become conscious is probably not by way of meditation (a dialogue with yourself) but when confronted by someone who is very aware what it means on a daily basis to be part of a minority caste in a world of male and white privilege.

If you are looking for a definition of a caste system, *New York Times* journalist and the first woman of African-American heritage to win the Pulitzer Prize in journalism, Isabel Wilkerson fills the void: "A caste system is an artificial construction, a fixed and embedded ranking of human value that sets the presumed supremacy of one group against the presumed inferiority of other groups on the basis of ancestry and often immutable traits, traits that would be neutral in the abstract but are ascribed life-and-death meaning."[125]

Caste and racism are neither synonymous nor mutually exclusive, so Wilkerson describes caste as the bones and race as the skin. She also adds a helpful picture: "As we go about our daily lives, caste is the wordless usher in a darkened theater, flashlight cast down the aisles, guiding us to our assigned seats for a performance."[126] In an interview, Wilkerson explained that her motivation for writing *Caste: The Origins of Our Discontents* was to expose the depths of dehumanization that goes beyond race and extends to other countries, such as India, where other contextual factors come into play. While Wilkerson does not invoke the original sin perspective, it is clear that the summer of discontent in America, 2020, disclosed a pent-up anger simmering for a lifetime of being treated as someone who is assigned to a lower class of human being.[127]

Was the Black Lives Matter uprising during the summer of 2020 destined to be yet another flash-in-the-pan kind of progress? Writing for *The Atlantic*, Mychal Denzel Smith admits that progress is progress, but real progress is really hard if you are up against "the behemoth of systematized oppression." He is correct that "incremental change keeps the grinding forces of oppression—of death—in place." He continues, "Actively advocating for this position is a moral failure."[128] Yet what Gandhi accomplished in India, what Mandela accomplished in South Africa, and what Martin Luther King Jr. achieved in America should not be counted as failures, just because they did not change human nature in a fundamental way. Unless human nature takes a radical turn toward our best self, the good fight will always be the long fight. This much is certain: we must be vigilant until our hearts are so transformed that every drop of racial hatred becomes a river of compassion.

I've been thinking about which of the Ten Commandments applies to white privilege and white fragility. (In this context, fragility refers to the reluctance to examine one's motives and behaviors because we know, deep down, the truth about ourselves is almost always painful.) Adam and Eve's banishment into the cold, cruel world signified the loss of innocence, but the world has changed—oh! how it has changed—for our version of a cold, cruel world is very different. Those Ten Commandments were Yahweh's way to bind together in covenantal relationship a people prone to forgetting who they were and what they were for. What God expects of them is black and white clear. You know if you didn't keep a Sabbath day, or profaned the name of God, or disrespected your elders, or murdered another person, or committed adultery, or stole something, or coveted what another has and you don't. Those commandants get to the root of the kind of sinful behavior that can make us feel guilty. Racism is different insofar as it has become an integral part of our history as a nation, and insofar as it has been hidden within the identity of straight white males. Prejudice is so subtle that it becomes established simply through homogeneity. Try confessing willful complicity as you gather to worship God.

Writing about the backlash that met the newly elected Barack Obama in Congress and the backlash that motivated white voters, Wilkerson writes: "Consciously or not, many white voters were 'seeking to reassert a racial order in which their group is firmly on the top.'"[129] Adding further clarification: This is a voting bloc that feels "the rug is being pulled out from under them—that the benefits they have enjoyed because of their race, their group's advantages, and their status atop the racial hierarchy are in jeopardy."[130] What intrigues me is how one accounts for sin as a description of human nature when our motivation might be not quite conscious. At what point is a highly evolved self-aware creature justified in using the word willful? Nevertheless, even though we go through life making many barely conscious decisions, I doubt if many of our significant decisions count as unaware. Certainly, voting is a moment where we should be consciously considering not only what is best for oneself but what is best for us.

> *Prayer*—O merciful God, we profess that we have seen and heard in the streets of our cities how much Black Lives Matter, as do all lives. We know. Yet we confess that we really don't know how it feels to live each day in the-shadow of a dominant white society. Amen. (Obviously this is a prayer of confession for predominantly white congregations.)

Artificial Technologies are by design ubiquitous and hidden. They guide your airplane to a safe landing and become indispensable when finding an address to a place you have never been. Therefore, be vigilant, because AI has the potential to change your life, your values, your reason for being without asking your permission.

Be vigilant, because whatever counts as sin will be written into the algorithms intended to relive you of the burden and responsibility of decisions you make about what your life is. We do have better things to do with our lives than staring at a screen! Your smart phone screen is not like your TV screen, for it really has become indispensable in so many ways. But there will come a time when you need to rethink what indispensable means, for the trajectory of this technology will be in only one direction. That would be in two words, *cheap bliss.*[131]

The AI of the future will be created to interface with you as a person: an android created in your own humanlike image. Throughout the world, programmers are busy teaching machines how to have common sense, how to match the correct facial expression with an emotion, and how to become a cherished companion. In Japan an increasing number of homes have a pet dog that does not need to be fed but barks and smiles just like a real dog, and in the near future, there will be companion androids for an ever-growing elderly population. So what is coming next?

The year is 2020 and the Chinese Communist Party understands why the future belongs to those who have the best AI technology and the most data.[132] Reminiscent of George Orwell's *Nineteen Eighty-Four* novel, "Big Brother is watching you" has arrived. China has already placed surveillance cameras in all key public places. China's general secretary Xi Jinping will not be satisfied until there is video coverage in *all* public places throughout the country. Those cameras will soon be able to match a picture identity with data that includes travel records, friends and associates, reading habits, purchases, and financial transactions. The stated purpose is to protect one billion people from security threats from within and without. But knowing what history shows us about power that corrupts, and knowing what has already happened to more than one million Uighurs who disappeared into concentration camps where their every move is watched, the world needs to be vigilant.[133]

An android has no skin in the game, as they say. The reason is quite simple. An android does not have a mortal body as we do, and therefore it can never experience the pain and joy of childbirth, the trials and fulfillment of aging, the thrill of victory and the agony of defeat, a lifetime of experiences as our body changes from childhood to adulthood, and all of the other pleasures that we experience through our five senses. With no skin in the game, an android cannot live a life measured by a beginning and an end, where the clock is always ticking and the years go by and the inevitable arrives. If the goal is to create androids in our image—and not everyone thinks this is a good idea—there should always be questions whether we can create anything not in our own image, because we are the ones doing the creating.

> *Prayer*—I love my smart phone and the way it is a portal to the world. I pray, though, that it does not diminish me, my values, my commitments, my reason for being the child of God that I am. Amen.

CRISPR is considered to be the most important scientific discovery of this century because it is the cheapest, simplest, and most effective way to manipulate DNA and RNA. CRISPR opens a world of unlimited possibilities. CRISPR has not yet reached the point where it can be used safely with cells as complex as those found in humans, but it has been readily used to edit genes of animals, such as mice modified to carry a specific abnormality and then tested against a possible cure. CRISPR will undoubtedly play a dominant role in re-engineering the food we eat by doing what is already being done, only more efficiently. It will be used to speed up the drug pipeline, since there is an insatiable appetite to enhance our bodies, our minds, and emotional states. But all of this does not compare to the possible medical benefits: combating HIV/AIDS, providing lifelong resistance to lipoprotein cholesterol (the bad cholesterol that is the leading cause of death worldwide), altering the DNA sequence to lower an individual's risk of cancer and diabetes, and increasing memory. The potential for CRISPR is so great that there are good reasons to believe it is our moral responsibility to move forward as quickly as possible. Moving forward at breakneck speed, though, is exactly what invites unintended consequences.

For every straightforward example of a medical enhancement, there is another that's more ambiguous (morally questionable). Once again, the question of equality is certain to come into play, for there will be some who can pay and some who cannot, and there will be disputes over what medical insurers will count as a necessity or an indulgence. One should also expect there to be unknown and unexpected tradeoffs, and this becomes so very important when you begin to alter the germ line, so a particular genetic change is inherited generation after generation. In 2008, the first CRISPR babies were born in China. A geneticist by the name of He Jiankui had altered the DNA of human embryos to make them HIV resistant and implanted them into a woman, who gave birth to twin girls. (If the HIV virus is not treated, and it is usually asymptomatic, it leads to AIDS.) As far as we know, these twins are alive and doing well. If these twins give birth to other children, they will have the same HIV resistance, but the rest of the story is yet to be told. We do know that altering this particular gene also increases the risk of West Nile fever, which is not a good thing for those living in a tropical climate. It should be noted that the worldwide scientific community's reaction was immediate and critical, calling for international guidelines to be established. Reading between the lines and knowing the nature of technology to push forward, the science of CRISPR will open the door to evolving ourselves.

Some of the reasons we should be hypervigilant in the twenty-first century should be evident, as we allow AI to dominate our lives and CRISPR to reorder life itself. But there is an underlying factor that is scarcely considered. These technologies, unlike any previous technologies, complicate and deepen our most important ethical decisions. What complicates them is the way they "mix obvious benefits with subtle harms in one seamless package."[134] Like no other technological advancement, CRISPR represents the epitome of this quandary. Those who suffer from sickle cell anemia are required to receive a blood transfusion on a regular basis, otherwise they die. A better solution, deleting the disease-causing letter A for the normal letter T, without disturbing the genome, is self-evident.

But the letter T is nature's way to protect us from malaria, so one must weigh the benefit against the gain. On a different front, CRISPR could be used to genetically modify some of us to be perfect astronauts and soldiers who feel no pain and have no fear of dying. As a tool that will be used to evolve ourselves, CRISPR has a way of creating a future we cannot see and don't want to see.

This last observation is from a biochemist who is trained to ask ethical questions. What was the chemist Paul Janssen considering when he created the synthetic opioid Fentanyl, with the subsequent decision by Janssen Pharmaceuticals to manufacture it? (Fentanyl is 50 to 100 times stronger than morphine.) Certainly they were aware of the obvious benefits, with subtle harms inherent in an opioid that had all the characteristics of morphine, as well as the ease and cost benefits of selling it as a miracle drug. The FDA did give its seal of approval, and Fentanyl was regarded as one of the most effective and safest medicines in the health care system to manage pain. Years later, we know the full story of an epidemic of devastating proportion, unconscionable greed, and a willingness by doctors to benefit from a scenario they chose not to envisage.

Speaking theologically and looking through the lens of original sin and original goodness, the call to be vigilant comes into focus, because it should compel us to consider at what cost we are doing this or that. And the word cost is the keystone, because the love of money and power are still the root of so much evil. Cost has a very different meaning for Christians, for their tradition speaks of the great cost of the love of the Creator-Father who gave his only Son to willingly die for us (John 3:16). And what is love without cost?

> Prayer—Gracious God, around us temptations abound. Some are obvious and some are subtle; all are insidious. Grant us wisdom and courage to see temptations for what they are—today, tomorrow, and in the years to come.

It does indeed seem to be our destiny to settle for nothing less than knowing all things. In the Anthropocene world we are creating, we have put aside childish ways of thinking in order to realize our full potential as an all-knowing creature. After all, our infinite potential is what gives our lives meaning, and our Promethean restlessness fuels our quest for greater knowledge. Is this really something we should associate with original sin?

Never before has *knowledge* become our greatest asset and our greatest temptation. Adam and Eve were tempted to possess knowledge of both good and evil. Whatever else that pairing meant, it signifies for us in this century that knowledge is power, control, and big business. To the extent that knowledge in its original context is the bait to open one's eyes and become all-powerful, little has changed and everything has changed.

We have become conditioned to think of knowledge as a good thing. In particular, we treasure empirical knowledge as the gold standard, because it has been wiped clean of subjectivity and prejudice. Empirical truth, however, is not something out there waiting to be objectively discovered. *The* truth is an abstraction. In practice, knowledge is inevitably constructed in our own image. This happens when raw data is reconstructed into information, and information becomes useful in some way for some people. But something else has transpired in the twenty-first century. Our technologies have become inordinately dependent upon data. The transition from analog to digital took place in such a short time because the latter had the distinct advantage of letting information be compressed, stored, and transmitted, in order to make it available to everyone. But digital data can be manipulated for both good and evil, in ways we are still discovering. Facebook is now the poster child for how a vision of enabling people of the world to communicate with each other became a tool for shaming, terrorizing, spreading fake news, controlling people, and just being mean to each other. *So be vigilant*, because as this century unfolds, there will be new technologies that begin with the best intentions, only to be corrupted by none other than the seven deadly sins of lust, gluttony, greed, sloth, anger, envy, and pride.

The twenty-first century will be both a continuation and an exacerbation of two converging factors: the dual potential of knowledge itself coupled with a species defined by antithetical dispositions to love and to hate. We are learning that many contemporary technologies have both unintended consequences and a dual use. The drilling for oil is associated with oil spills (an unintended consequence). The design of airplanes is associated with transporting passengers and bombs (dual use). The gun is an example of both converging factors. Do we blame the shooter or the gun? Both, because the shooter can't be trusted, and the nature of the knowledge used to develop an instrument for killing is hardly neutral. The one holding the gun is a human being who knows right from wrong and sometimes does the former, sometimes the latter. As our knowledge of how things work has grown, so has the potential for good and evil. Whether we are considering the bow and arrow or the gun, their dual use is blatant. It is not incidental that a simple rifle meant to kill a rabbit becomes an AK-47 assault rifle, considered to be the deadliest and most pervasive weapon in the history of military armament. The theoretical knowledge of the atom becomes both an atomic bomb to destroy a city and a nuclear reactor to light our cities. CRISPR might very well enable us to rid the world of a host of terrible genetic diseases and give birth to genetically modified individuals with an IQ of 170 who can create the next best thing or the next worst thing.

> *Prayer*—O Holy One, you have gifted us with minds to understand the universe, and so much more, and yet, it seems, we cannot abide the responsibility that comes with knowledge that is too good not to be exploited. Amen.

If everything goes as it should, data will become information, information will become knowledge, and knowledge will become wisdom. We have known for a long time that we have little enthusiasm to know the truth about ourselves, and yet wisdom is born of a realistic assessment of human nature. Chiseled into the forecourt of the temple of Apollo at Delphi were two words: "Know thyself." They were there to call worshipers to a reckoning with themselves before asking something of the gods. Today they bear a broader implication. They call us to consider the beautiful and ugly truths about ourselves. To neglect this responsibility is to suffer the consequences. One could say the game has changed, but the players are still the same. That would be a good way to acknowledge the efficacy of original sin.

The unique quality about wisdom is how it is associated with maturity. Knowledge becomes wisdom when those who handle it know that it can heat a home or burn it down.

Those who are wise are vigilant, because they understand human nature will always be an intricate mix of good intentions alongside bad intentions, embodied within a willful self. Those who are vigilant will look to enduring truths, because while they seem passé, they embody the kind of knowing we dare not live without.

RECOMMENDED READING

Bloomberg, Michael, and Carl Pope. *Climate of Hope: How Cities, Businesses, and Citizens Can Save the Planet.* New York: St. Martin's Press, 2017.

Doudna, Jennifer A., and Samuel H. Sternberg. *A Crack in Creation: Gene Editing and the Unthinkable Power to Control Evolution.* Boston: Houghton Mifflin Harcourt, 2017.

Enriques, Juan, and Steve Gullans. *Evolving Ourselves: How Unnatural Selection and Nonrandom Mutation Are Changing Life on Earth.* New York: Current/ Penguin, 2015.

"Human Nature." NOVA season 47, episode 11. https://www.pbs.org/video/ nova-human-nature-hcwiwk/. This program explains how CRISPR works and explores the social and moral implications.

Isaacson, Walter. *The Code Breaker: Jennifer Doudna: Gene Editing and the Future of the Human Race.* New York: Simon & Schuster, 2021.

Kanaan, Michael. *T–Minus AI: Humanity's Countdown to Artificial Intelligence and the New Pursuit of Global Power.* Dallas: BenBella, 2020.

Ian McEwan. *Machines Like Me and People Like You.* New York: Penguin Random, 2019.

Tegmark, Mark. *Life 3.0: Being Human in the Age of Artificial Intelligence.* New York: Alfred Knopf, 2017.

Webb, Amy. *The Big Nine: How the Tech Titans and Their Thinking Machines Could Warp Humanity.* New York: Public Affairs, 2019.

Wilkerson, Isabel. *Caste: The Origins of Our Discontents.* New York: Random House, 2020.

Endnotes

CHAPTER 1

1. Coleman, *Eden's Garden*, 86–89, 113–21.
2. Harari, *Homo Deus*, 47.
3. Harari, *Homo Deus*, 49–55, and ch. 11, "The Data Religion."
4. Harari, *Homo Deus*, 49–55.
5. Harari, *Home Deus*, 271.

6. Harari, *Homo Deus*, 271.
7. Wasik, "So the Internet Didn't Turn Out."
8. Most of us know that we have not yet created machines with minds and wills. Some believe we might. For the moment, I agree with Mark Halpen, who knows way more than I do about AI. He argues convincingly that computers merely execute a program, and we are likely to buy into the "specter of autonomy." See Halpern, "No Ghost in the Machine."
9. For a more complete survey of how science dethroned theology and became the dominant provider of truths that matter, see Coleman, *State of Affairs*.
10. Van Huyssteen's Gifford Lectures, *Alone in the World*, 161–62.
11. Van Huyssteen, *Alone in the World*, 162.
12. Taylor, *Speaking of Sin*, 5–6.
13. See Bill Chappell, reporter for NPR, "This Is All Wrong."
14. Writing from a much broader perspective of sacred texts, Karen Armstrong concludes her magisterial book *The Lost Art of Scripture* with thoughts concerning our contemporary propensity to misuse and misinterpret scriptures (451–82).
15. Alter, *Art of Biblical Narrative*, 193.
16. Ellul, *Humiliation of the Word*, 28. Twenty-one years later, Walter Brueggemann sounded a similar prophetic voice in *The Word That Redescribes the World*.
17. Greenblatt, *Rise and Fall*, 3–4.

CHAPTER 2

18. Alter, *Art of Biblical Narrative*, 177.
19. Davis, *Scripture, Culture, and Agriculture*, 29.
20. Von Rad, *Genesis*, 86–87.
21. Van Huyssteen, *Alone in the World*, 132–45.
22. Harari, *Homo Deus,* 20.
23. Greenblatt, *Rise and Fall*, ch. 14, "Darwin's Doubts."
24. Greenblatt, *Rise and Fall,* 634.
25. Greenblatt, *Rise and Fall*, 61–62
26. Van Huyssteen, *Alone in the World*, 97.
27. Barth, *Epistle to the Romans*, 250.
28. For an expansive exploration of the meaning of cave drawings, see Van Huyssteen, *Alone in the World*, chs. 4 and 5. The depiction of a wild pig, outlined and filled in with mulberry-hued pigment, may date back to at least 45,000 years, making it the oldest figurative art discovered. See Ferreira, "Pig Painting."
29. Niebuhr, *Nature and Destiny*, 1:251–52.
30. Mark Smith is determined to separate a fall and a doctrine of original sin from a close reading of Gen 3–4 and 6. He argues that these chapters "dramatize what the doctrine of original sin *attributes* to Genesis 3" (Smith, *Genesis*, 7; italics added).
31. Robinson, *Death of Adam*, 240.
32. As paraphrased from Robinson, *Death of Adam*, 240.
33. Alter, *Art of Biblical Narrative*, 219–20.

CHAPTER 3

34. Wiley, *Original Sin*, 3–4.
35. Christian Reformed Church, "Canons of Dort."
36. Niebuhr, *Nature and Destiny*, 1:269.
37. Niebuhr, *Nature and Destiny,* 1:122. In a more poetic way, Niebuhr writes: "Humanity has not only a rational faculty but also an imagination which surveys the heavens, aspires to the stars and breaks all the little systems of prudence which the mind constructs" (Niebuhr, *Beyond Tragedy*, 161).
38. Calvin, *Institutes*, 1.15.4.
39. Christian Reformed Church, "Canons of Dort"; italics added.
40. Wolterstorff, *Hearing the Call*, 8–9.
41. Marty, "Is the Destruction of Monuments."

CHAPTER 4

42. Prothero, *God Is Not One*, 136.
43. Bernard of Clairvaux, "O Sacred Head."

44. Robinson, *Givenness of Things*, 256.

45. Darwin, *Descent of Man*, 105.

46. De Waal, *Bonobo and the Atheist*, 36. Here de Waal is citing Huxley, *Life and Letters of Thomas Henry Huxley* (New York: Appleton, 1916), 2:322. De Waal has his own explanation why the process of natural selection does not ipso facto produce nasty results (see his ch. 3, "Goodness Explained").

47. Tomasello, *Why We Cooperate*, and in much greater detail, *Becoming Human*.

48. Bloom, *Just Babies*, 8.

49. *Bloom, Just Babies*, 27.

50. Bloom, *Just Babies*, 5, 106–14.

51. See Wrangham, who develops this argument about our evolution by way of domesticating ourselves in *The Goodness Paradox*.

52. Desmond and Moore, *Darwin's Sacred Cause*.

53. A very helpful overview of the leading theories about Neanderthal and the displacement of this species by modern humans can be found in Klein, "Great Human Odyssey," from the NOVA PBS series.

54. In *The Rational Optimist*, the indefatigable Matt Ridley argues that human nature has not changed, but human culture has; and it really changed when modern human beings found ways to link minds and accumulate knowledge.

55. Luther, "A Mighty Fortress."

56. Volf, *Exclusion and Embrace*, 89–90.

57. Zusak, *Book Thief*, 934.

58. Damasio, *Stranger Order of Things*, 224.

59. Ricoeur, *Symbolism of Evil*, 253.

60. Niebuhr, *Nature and Destiny of Man*, 1:261–63. In three pages, Niebuhr registers his theological reasons why a historical-literalistic reading of the Adam and Eve narrative is misguided and not helpful in a modern mindset.

61. Greenblatt, *Rise and Fall*, 108–12.

62. Rousseau, *Emile*, 37.

63. Neiman, *Evil in Modern Thought*, 43, 106–7.

64. Niebuhr, *Nature and Destiny*, 1:242.

65. Bregman, *Humankind*, 27.

66. This often repeated sentiment is attributed to the defense attorney Bryan Stevenson, who has dedicated his career as a lawyer to represent those unjustly convicted, including Walter McMillian, wrongfully imprisoned and sentenced to death. A book and a film entitled *Just Mercy* tell this story.

CHAPTER 5

67. The doctrine of original justice is principally a Roman Catholic teaching that refers to attributes of holiness and justice enjoyed by Adam and Eve before the fall.

68. Barth, *Doctrine of Creation*, 4.

69. Barth, *Doctrine of Creation*, 4.

70. When we consider the neglect of an ecological perspective in Christian theology, one seminal book comes to mind: Santmire, *Travail of Nature*.

71. Crichton and Koepp, "Jurassic Park."

72. Barth, *Doctrine of Creation*, 149.

73. Johnson, *Ask the Beasts*, 277.

74. Johnson, *Ask the Beasts*, 269–73.

75. Hart, *Aesthetics of Christian Truth*, 17.

76. Hart, *Aesthetics of Christian Truth*, 4, 132, 407.

77. Safina, *Becoming Wild*, 204.

78. Safina, *Becoming Wild*, 205.

79. Among other books that detail the devastation that awaits us, see Wallace-Wells, *Uninhabitable Earth*.

80. Lightman, *Searching for Stars*, 6.

81. For an excellent discussion of natural law, both past and present, see Porter, *Natural and Divine Law*. A particularly relevant section is in 224–34.

82. Mouw, *He Shines*.

83. Macmillan, as cited in Shuttleworth, "Theosis: Partaking of the Divine Nature" at ww1.antochian.org/content/theosis-partaking-divine-nature. In addition, see Fairbairn, "Salvation as Theosis."

84. For an excellent depiction of how dirt can literally save our planet, see Tickell, dirs., *Kiss the Ground*, a Netflix documentary.

CHAPTER 6

85. I noticed this sign as part of a video during the singing of "I Am Open and I Am Willing" by Holly Near. See https://www.youtube.com/watch?v=tnmRoNeezWA&feature=emb_logo.

86. Niebuhr, *Nature and Destiny*, 1:270.

87. Taylor, *Speaking of Sin*, 62.

88. Niebuhr, *Nature and Destiny*, 1:182–83.

89. Niebuhr, *Nature and Destiny*, 1:290.

90. Niebuhr, *Nature and Destiny*, 1:183.

91. Niebuhr, *Nature and Destiny*, 1:183.

92. Brueggemann, *Finally Comes the Poet*, 98.

93. Brueggemann, *Finally Comes the Poet*, 107.

94. Brueggemann, *Finally Comes the Poet*, 69–70.

95. Julian, "Childhood in an Anxious Age," 28–39.

96. Here—in this description of our redeemed life in Christ where sin has become an impossible possibility—I am following the exegesis of Beker, *Paul the Apostle*, 216–17. How to interpret Rom 7 is a perennial problem, but it need not be one. As Beker points out, Rom 7:7–25 serves as a bridge between Rom 6 (6:1—"I am speaking in human terms because of your natural limitations")

and Rom 8 (8:3—"who walk not according to the flesh but according to the Spirit").

97. See the opinion piece by Bruenig, "Racism Makes a Liar."

98. Niebuhr, *Nature and Destiny*, 1:279.

99. David Brooks, as cited by Ellie, "Man for All Reasons." This article contains a penetrating analysis into how Niebuhr proved to be the iconoclast who annoyed just about everyone.

100. See Noble, "Irony."

101. For an equally graphic, up-close voyage into the hell of Rwanda, as told by someone called to serve as commander of the UN Assistance Mission to keep the peace, read Lieutenant-General Roméo Dallaire's *Shake Hands With the Devil*.

102. Rhodes, *World as It Is*, 18–19.

103. This quote is how Samantha Power ends her book, *Education of an Idealist*.

104. Niebuhr, *Nature and Destiny*, 2:43.

105. Niebuhr, *Children of Light*, xi.

106. Stone, *Reinhold Niebuhr*, 140.

107. Rice, "Niebuhr's Critique of Religion in America," in *Reinhold Niebuhr Revisited*, 318.

108. Ellie, "Man for all Reasons."

109. King, "From the Birmingham Jail."

110. The inspiration for announcing something that seems to appear out of nowhere is Stephen King's story "The Life of Chuck" in *If It Bleeds*.

111. Diane Ackerman is eloquent in her description of what "the hand of man is everywhere" looks like in *The Human Age*.

112. Purdy, "Billion Dollar Burger."

113. Enriquez and Gullans, *Evolving Ourselves*, 140.

114. Padawer, "Two-Minus-One Pregnancy."

115. Zhang, "Last Children of Down Syndrome."

116. Zhang, "Last Children of Down Syndrome," 46.

117. Zhang, "Last Children of Down Syndrome."

118. Enriquez and Gullans, *Evolving Ourselves*, 206.

119. Bess, *Our Grandchildren Redesigned*, 74–83.

120. See Lustgarten, "Refugees from the Earth."

121. Klein, *On the (Burning) Case*, 133.

122. Weiss, "Fight to Nullify."

123. Burns, dir., *Not for Ourselves Alone*.

124. Morrison, "A Humanist View," as cited in "Twelve of Toni Morrison's."

125. Wilkerson, *Caste*, 17.

126. Wilkerson, *Caste*, 17.

127. Interview by Paul, "Isabel Wilkerson Talks About 'Caste.'" Also, see Garner, "Isabel Wilkerson's 'Caste.'"

128. Smith "Police Reform Is Not Enough," 14–17.

129. Wilkerson, *Caste*, 326.

130. Wilkerson, *Caste*, 328. Here Wilkerson is citing Jardina, *White Identity Politics*, 272, 267.

131. For a comprehensive examination of what cheap bliss looks like, see Frischmann and Selinger, *Re-Engineering Humanity*, 102–23.

132. The themes of "who has the most data controls the world" and "the world needs to be vigilant" are clearly presented in two important books: Amy Webb, *The Big Nine,* and Michael Kanaan, *T-Minus AI.* The latter book also includes a history and a clear explanation of machine-learning.

133. Andersen, "When China Sees All," 59–68.

134. Fukuyama, *Our Posthuman Future*, 7.

Bibliography

Ackerman, Diane. *The Human Age: The World Shaped by Us*. New York: W. W. Norton, 2014.

Alter, Robert. *The Art of Biblical Narrative*. New York: Basic, 2011.

Andersen, Ross. "When China Sees All." *Atlantic* (Sept. 2020) 59–68.

Armstrong, Karen. *The Lost Art of Scripture: Rescuing the Sacred Texts*. New York: Alfred A. Knopf, 2019.

Barth, Karl. "The Doctrine of Creation," *Church Dogmatics*, III. 2. Edited by G. W. Bromiley & T. F. Torrance, translated by Harold Knight et al. Church Dogmatics III/2. Edinburgh: T. & T. Clark, 1960.

———. *The Epistle to the Romans*. Translated from the 6th ed. by Edwyn C. Hoskyns. Oxford: Oxford University Press, 1968.

Beker, Christiaan J. *Paul the Apostle: The Triumph of God in Life and Thought*. Philadelphia: Fortress, 1980.

Bernard of Clairvaux. "O Sacred Head, Now Wounded." Translated by James W. Alexander. https://hymnary.org/text/o_sacred_head_now_wounded.

Bess, Michael. *Our Grandchildren Redesigned: Life in the Bioengineered Society of the Near Future*. Boston: Beacon, 2015.

Bloom, Paul. *Just Babies: The Origins of Good and Evil*. New York: Crown, 2013.

Bloomberg, Michael, and Carl Pope. *Climate of Hope: How Cities, Businesses, and Citizens Can Save the Planet*. New York: St. Martin's Press, 2017.

Bregman, Rutger. *Humankind: A Hopeful History*. Translated by Erica Moore and Elizabeth Manton. New York: Little, Brown, 2019. iBooks.

Brueggemann, Walter. *Finally Comes the Poet: Daring Speech for Proclamation*. Minneapolis: Fortress, 1989.

———. *The Word That Redescribes the World: The Bible and Discipleship*. Minneapolis: Fortress, 2006.

Bruenig, Elizabeth. "Racism Makes a Liar of God." *New York Times*, Aug. 9, 2020.

Burns, Ken, dir. *Not for Ourselves Alone: The Story of Elizabeth Cady Stanton and Susan B. Anthony*. Washington, DC: Florentine Films and WETA, 1999.

Bibliography

Calvin, John. *Institutes of the Christian Religion*. Edited by John T McNeill. Library of Christian Classics. 2 vols. Philadelphia: Westminster Press, 1960.

Chappell, Bill. "'This Is All Wrong,' Greta Thunberg Tells World Leaders at U. N. Climate Session." NPR, Sept. 23, 2019. https://www.npr.org/2019/09/23/763389015/this-is-all-wrong-greta-thunberg-tells-world-leaders-at-u-n-climate-session.

Christian Reformed Church. "The Canons of Dort." www.crcna.org/welcome/beliefs/confessions/canons-dort.

Coleman, Richard J. *Eden's Garden: Rethinking Sin and Evil in an Era of Scientific Promise*. Lanham, MD: Rowman & Littlefield, 2007.

———. *State of Affairs: The Science-Theology Controversy*. Eugene, OR: Cascade, 2014.

Crichton, Michael and David Koepp. "Jurassic Park." Directed by Steven Spielberg. Universal City, CA: Amblin Entertainment, 1993.

Dallaire, Roméo. *Shake Hands With the Devil: The Failure of Humanity in Rwanda*. Toronto: Random House Canada, 2003.

Damasio, Antonio. *The Strange Order of Things*. New York, Vintage, 2018.

Darwin, Charles. *The Descent of Man, and Selection in Relation to Sex*. Princeton, NJ: Princeton University Press, 1981.

Davis, Ellen. *Scripture, Culture, and Agriculture: An Agrarian Reading of the Bible*. New York: Cambridge University Press, 2009.

Dawkins, Richard. *The Selfish Gene*. New York: Oxford University Press, 1976.

de Waal, Frans B. M. *The Bonobo and the Atheist: In Search of Humanism Among the Primates*. New York: W. W. Norton, 2013.

Desmond, Adrian, and James Moore. *Darwin's Sacred Cause: Race, Slavery and the Quest for Human Origins*. Boston: Houghton Mifflin Harcourt, 2009.

Doudna, Jennifer A., and Samuel H. Sternberg. *A Crack in Creation: Gene Editing and the Unthinkable Power to Control Evolution*. Boston: Houghton Mifflin Harcourt, 2017.

Ellie, Paul. "A Man for all Reasons." *Atlantic* (Nov. 2007). https://www.theatlantic.com/magazine/archive/2007/11/a-man-for-all-reasons/306337/.

Ellul, Jacques. *Humiliation of the Word*. Grand Rapids: Eerdmans, 1985.

Enriques, Juan, and Steve Gullans. *Evolving Ourselves: How Unnatural Selection and Nonrandom Mutation Are Changing Life on Earth*. New York: Current/Penguin, 2015.

Fairbairn, Donald. "Salvation as Theosis: The Teaching of Eastern Orthodoxy." https://www.thegospelcoalition.org/themelios/article/salvation-as-theosis-the-teaching-of-eastern-orthodoxy/.

Ferreira, Becky. "Pig Painting May Be World's Oldest Cave Art Yet." *New York Times,* Jan. 13, 2021.

Fredriksen, Paula. *Sin: The Early History of an Idea*. Princeton, NJ: Princeton University Press, 2012.

Frischmann, Brett, and Evan Selinger. *Re-Engineering Humanity*. Cambridge, UK: Cambridge University Press, 2018.

Bibliography

Fukuyama, Francis. *Our Posthuman Future.* New York: Farrar, Straus & Giroux, 2002.

Garner, Dwight. "Isabel Wilkerson's 'Caste' Is an 'Instant American Classic' about Our Abiding Sin." *New York Times,* July 31, 2020.

Gilkey, Langdon. *On Niebuhr: A Theological Study.* Chicago: University of Chicago Press, 2001.

"Great Human Odyssey." NOVA season 43, episode 12. https://www.pbs.org/video/nova-great-human-odyssey/.

Greenblatt, Stephen. *The Rise and Fall of Adam and Eve: The Story That Created Us.* New York: Norton, 2017. iBooks.

Halpern, Mark. "No Ghost in the Machine." *American Scholar* (Spring 2020) 20–31. https://theamericanscholar.org/no-ghost-in-the-machine/.

Harari, Yuval Noah. *Homo Deus: A Brief History of Tomorrow.* New York: HarperCollins, 2017.

Hart, David Bentley. *The Beauty of the Infinite: The Aesthetics of Christian Truth.* Grand Rapids: Eerdmans, 2003.

"Human Nature." NOVA season 47, episode 11. https://www.pbs.org/video/nova-human-nature-ga2gau/.

Isaacson, Walter. *The Code Breaker: Jennifer Doudna: Gene Editing and the Future of the Human Race.* New York: Simon & Schuster, 2021.

Jacobs, Alan. *Original Sin: A Cultural History.* New York: HarperOne, 2008.

Jahren, Hope. *The Story of More: How We Got to Climate Change and Where to Go from Here.* New York: Vintage, 2020.

Jardina, Ashley. *White Identity Politics.* Cambridge Studies in Public Opinion and Political Psychology. Cambridge, UK: Cambridge University Press, 2019.

Johnson, Elizabeth A. *Ask the Beasts: Darwin and the God of Love.* London: Bloomsbury, 2014.

Julian, Kate. "Childhood in an Anxious Age." *Atlantic* (May 2020) 28–39.

Kanaan, Michael. *T-Minus AI: Humanity's Countdown to Artificial Intelligence and the New Pursuit of Global Power.* Dallas: BenBella, 2020.

King, Martin Luther, Jr. "From the Birmingham Jail." *Christian Century* 80 (June 12, 1963) 767–73.

King, Stephen. *If It Bleeds: New Fiction.* New York: Scribner, 2020.

Klein, Larry. "Great Human Odyssey." NOVA, season 43, episode 12. Aired Oct. 5, 2016, PBS. https://www.pbs.org/wgbh/nova/video/great-human-odyssey/.

Klein, Naomi. *On the (Burning) Case for a Green New Deal.* New York: Simon & Schuster, 2019.

Lightman, Alan. *Searching for Stars on an Island in Maine.* New York: Vintage, 2018.

Lustgarten, Abraham. "Refugees from the Earth." *New York Times,* July 26, 2020.

Luther, Martin. "A Mighty Fortress Is Our God." Translated by Frederick H. Hedge. https://hymnary.org/text/a_mighty_fortress_is_our_god_a_bulwark.

Bibliography

Macmillan, as cited in Shuttleworth, "Theosis: Partaking of the Divine Nature" at ww1.antiochian.org/content/theosis-partaking-divine-nature.

Marty, Peter W. "Is the Destruction of Monuments a Rewriting of History?" *Christian Century* (July 13, 2020) 3.

McEwan, Ian. *Machines Like Me and People Like You*. New York: Penguin Random, 2019.

Moltmann, Jürgen. *The Crucified God: The Cross of Christ as the Foundation and Criticism of Christian Theology*. London: SCM, 1974.

Morrison, Toni. "Twelve of Toni Morrison's Most Memorable Quotes." *New York Times*, Aug. 6, 2019. https://www.nytimes.com/2019/08/06/books/toni-morrison-quotes.html.

Mouw, Richard J. *He Shines in All That's Fair*. Grand Rapids: Eerdmans, 2001.

Neiman, Susan. *Evil in Modern Thought: An Alternative History of Philosophy*. Princeton, NJ: Princeton University Press, 2002.

Niebuhr, Reinhold. *Beyond Tragedy: Essays on the Christian Interpretation of History*. New York: Scribner's, 1937.

———. *The Children of Light, and the Children of Darkness*. New York: Charles Scribner's Sons, 1944.

———. *The Nature and Destiny of Man*. 2 vols. New York: Scribner's, 1941.

Noble, David W. "'Irony' in Reinhold Niebuhr's Irony of American History." In *Reinhold Niebuhr Revisited*, edited by Daniel F. Rice, 302–16. Grand Rapids: Eerdmans, 2009.

Padawer, Ruth. "The Two-Minus-One Pregnancy." *New York Times Magazine*, Aug. 10, 2011.

Paul, Pamela. Interview, "Isabel Wilkerson Talks About Caste.'" New York Times. Aug. 7, 2020.

Pinker, Steven. *The Better Angels of Our Nature*. New York: Penguin/Viking, 2013.

Porter, Jean. *Natural and Divine Law*. Grand Rapids: Eerdmans, 1999.

Power, Samantha. *The Education of an Idealist: A Memoir*. New York: Dey Street/William Morrow, 2020.

———. *A Problem From Hell: America and the Age of Genocide*. New York: Basic, 2002.

Prothero, Stephen. *God Is Not One*. New York: HarperOne, 2011.

Purdy, Chase. "Billion Dollar Burger: Inside Big Tech's Race for the Future of Food." *New York Times*, June 16, 2020.

Rad, Gerhard von. *Genesis*. Philadelphia: Westminster, 1961.

Rhodes, Ben. *The World as It Is: A Memoir of the Obama White House*. New York: Random House, 2018.

Rice, Daniel R., ed. *Reinhold Niebuhr: Revisited*. Grand Rapids: Eerdmans, 2009.

Ricoeur, Paul. *The Symbolism of Evil*. Translated by Emerson Buchanan. Boston: Beacon, 1967.

Ridley, Matt. *The Rational Optimist: How Prosperity Evolves*. New York: Harper/Perennial, 2011.

Bibliography

Robinson, Marilynne. *The Death of Adam: Essays on Modern Thought*. Boston: Houghton Mifflin, 1998.

———. *The Givenness of Things: Essays*. New York: Farrar, Straus & Giroux, 2015.

Rousseau, Jean-Jacques. *Emile, or On Education*. Translated by Alan Bloom. New York: Basic Books, 1979.

Safina, Carl. *Becoming Wild: How Animal Cultures Raise Families, Create Beauty, and Achieve Peace*. New York: Henry Holt, 2020.

———. *Beyond Words: What Animals Think and Feel*. New York: Henry Holt, 2015.

Sands, Kathleen M. *Escape From Paradise: Evil and Tragedy in Feminist Theology*. Minneapolis: Fortress, 1994.

Santmire, H. Paul. *The Travail of Nature: The Ambiguous Ecological Promise of Christian Theology*. Philadelphia: Fortress, 1985.

Sheets-Johnstone, Maxine. *The Roots of Morality*. University Park, PA: Pennsylvania State University Press, 2008.

Shuttleworth, Mark. "Theosis: Partaking of the Divine Nature." http://ww1.antiochian.org/content/theosis-partaking-divine-nature.

Smith, Mark S. *The Genesis of Good and Evil: The Fall(out) and Original Sin in the Bible*. Louisville, KY: Westminster John Knox, 2019.

Smith, Mychal Denzel. "Police Reform Is Not Enough." *Atlantic* (Sept. 2020) 14–17.

Stevenson, Bryan. *Just Mercy: A Story of Justice and Redemption*. New York: Spiegel & Grau, 2014.

Stone, Ronald H. *Reinhold Niebuhr: Prophet to Politicians*. New York: Abingdon, 1972.

Taylor, Barbara Brown. *Speaking of Sin: The Lost Language of Salvation*. Cambridge, MA: Cowley, 2000.

Tegmark, Mark. *Life 3.0: Being Human in the Age of Artificial Intelligence*. New York: Alfred Knopf, 2017.

Tickell, Rebecca and Josh, dirs. *Kiss the Ground*. Netflix. Ojai, CA: Big Picture Ranch, 2020.

Tomasello, Michael. *Becoming Human: A Theory of Ontogeny*. Cambridge, MA: Belknap, 2019.

———. *Why We Cooperate*. Cambridge, MA: MIT Press, 2009.

Van Huyssteen, Wentzel J. *Alone in the World?: Human Uniqueness in Science and Theology*. Gifford Lectures. Grand Rapids: Eerdmans, 2006.

Volf, Miroslav. *Exclusion and Embrace: A Theological Exploration of Identity, Otherness, and Reconciliation*. Nashville: Abingdon, 1996.

Wallace-Wells, David. *The Uninhabitable Earth: Life After Warming*. New York: Duggan, 2019.

Wasik, Bill. "So the Internet Didn't Turn Out the Way We Hoped." *New York Times Magazine*, Nov. 17, 2019.

Webb, Amy. *The Big Nine: How the Tech Titans and Their Thinking Machines Could Warp Humanity*. New York: Public Affairs, 2019.

Bibliography

Weiss, Elaine. "The Fight to Nullify the Nineteenth Amendment." *New York Times*, Aug. 30, 2020.

Wiley, Tatha. *Original Sin: Origins, Developments, Contemporary Meanings*. New York: Paulist, 2002.

Wilkerson, Isabel. *Caste: The Origins of Our Discontents*. New York: Random House, 2020.

Wolterstorff, Nicholas. *Hearing the Call: Liturgy, Justice, Church, and the World*. Grand Rapids: Eerdmans, 2011.

Wrangham, Richard. *The Goodness Paradox: The Strange Relationship Between Virtue and Violence*. New York: Vintage, 2009.

Zhang, Sarah. "The Last Children of Down Syndrome." *Atlantic* (Dec. 2020) 42–55.

Zusak, Markus. *The Book Thief*. New York: Knopf, 2005.

Made in the USA
Las Vegas, NV
11 March 2023

68917156R00069